G000151960

THE JEWI___
WAY OF LIFE

BY

RABBI DAVID ARONSON

The National Academy for Adult Jewish Studies
3080 BROADWAY, NEW YORK CITY

COPYRIGHT, 1946, BY

The Jewish Theological Seminary of America

PRINTED IN THE UNITED STATES OF AMERICA
BY THE VAIL-BALLOU PRESS, INC., BINGHAMTON, N. Y.

To My Father and to
the Memory of My Mother

"There are three partners in man: the Holy One Blessed Be He, the father and the mother. When one honors one's parents God considers it as a tribute to Him."

Kid. 30b

To My Wife

"To gain a good wife is to gain a fortune, a boon bestowed by the Eternal."

Prov. 18:21

To My Sons

"That you may walk in the way of good men, and keep the paths of the righteous."

Prov. 2:20

The tradition of our parents, the spirit of our home, the sense of responsibility for our children, are three pillars which mark the Jewish Way of Life.

Introduction

The broad purpose of adult Jewish education in our time must be to restore to the minds of American Jews the basic ideals of Jewish life so as to guide, discipline and dominate their lives as individuals and as a collective group. This volume, "The Jewish Way of Life" by Rabbi David Aronson, earnestly attempts to serve this great purpose. The author seeks to impart in popular form some of the great concepts of the Jewish religious tradition, and strives to implant the desire to pursue them. Books of this character are in keeping with our cultural heritage. When Rabbi Isaac Aboab wrote his Menorat Ha-Maor (The Lamp of Illumination) or when Rabbi Elijah di Vidas wrote his Reshit Hochmah (The Beginning of Wisdom) they each sought in their way to enlighten the minds and to stimulate the will of their readers so as to further the continuance of the glorious tradition of the Jewish people. It is hoped that in a modest way Rabbi Aronson's book will add wisdom and light the way for American Israel today.

This volume was written to serve the needs of adult students who can devote about eight or ten sessions in any one semester to Jewish studies. It is one of a series of many texts already published and others which are to be published by the National Academy for Adult Jewish Studies. It is hoped that these publications will help to create a purposeful and strong American Jewish community.

ISRAEL M. GOLDMAN
Director, National Academy
for Adult Jewish Studies.

Shevat 5706
January 1946

Preface

There is a story told of a gay and far from pious Southern colonel whose servant was a staunch believer in the Calvinistic doctrine of Predestination or Election. One day the colonel asked him whether he thought that his master was among the elect. "Well, Sir," the servant replied, "I never heard of anyone elected who was not a candidate."

No one lives consistently on the high level of one's lofty ideals. This is as true of peoples as of individuals. But no one can rise above his ideals. The ideals of a people at any time are the upper limits to which a people can rise. There are many factors which determine whether a people retains or attains its cherished position. But no people can attain or long retain that position unless it cherishes that position as its ideal and is so-to-speak a candidate anxious to hold that position.

When we present the thoughts and activities outlined in this volume as Jewish, it is not because they were necessarily first conceived or practiced by this or that individual Jew, but rather because they were accepted as ideals by what Dr. Solomon Schechter called catholic Israel —the historic conscience of the Jewish people, of *Klal Yisroel*.

People may backslide from the ideal but as long as they do not repudiate the ideal *per se*, there is hope for them. There is something one can appeal to. One can argue with the backsliders showing them how far they have drifted from their accepted ideal. There is hope for a reformation and a new effort to live up to the ideal.

This has been the history of Israel. From the very beginning it accepted as its ideal the will of a universal God of justice and righteousness in whose image man is created and according to whose will man is to regulate his life. However often the practices of the individual Jew fell short of this ideal, there was always the challenge of the historic conscience of his people which accepted this ideal and which called him to repentance and regeneration. This is the moral force which marked

vii

Israel as unique in the pagan world which surrounded him in the course of his long history. This is his greatest contribution to the basic moral forces struggling for realization in the world today—struggling against the Nazi ideologies.

For the greatest moral danger of Nazism is not that it is ruthlessly brutal in its practices but that it is ruthlessly brutal in its thoughts—that it has brutality as an ideal. On the other hand the greatness of America is not that it is already "the land of the free" but that there exists the will to be known as and to become the land of the free. Its greatness lies in the fact that it has accepted as its foundation-stone the Judaeo-Christian concept that "all men are created equal and are endowed by their Creator with certain inalienable rights." Aspiring to such an ideal, America will gradually reach the position of freedom for all in its own borders and will make its great contribution to the establishment of a free world.

In this new, free world for which we are fighting, the Judaeo-Christian tradition will play a leading role. This volume is an endeavor to point out, in a limited way, some of the phases of the Jewish contribution to this moral partnership. It covers but a fraction of the rich field of Jewish thought and gives but a glimpse of what Judaism considers the ideal way of life. Incidentally, to the Jew, thought and conduct must be mated. *Lo HaMidrash Ikor Elo Hamaase,* "not the theoretical discussion but its practical application" is what determines moral life. On the other hand, *"Lo Am Haaretz Hasid,"* "the ignorant man cannot be pious." Proper conduct results from proper thoughts and from the consciousness of high ideals and principles. To the Jew high thoughts are the roots and moral conduct is the fruit of the Tree of Life.

Jewish thought and Jewish conduct did lead to the Tree of Life. This is the testimony of history. As long as Israel followed in these paths, as long as he was sensitive to these ideals, he not only survived the antagonistic forces and the persecutions of the centuries but he survived on a high spiritual and cultural plane. *"Ve'hi she'amda lonu."* This has ever been the source of our strength. This is our glorious tradition.

I am grateful to Doctor Israel M. Goldman, who from the beginning suggested and encouraged this work. I am also thankful to him and to

Doctor Simon Greenberg for their patience in reading the manuscript and for their many valuable suggestions and technical assistance.

DAVID ARONSON

Minneapolis, Minn.
Tammuz, 5705; July, 1945.

Contents

CHAPTER I

Starting the Day Right

1. *Life is purposeful*

One's ideal in the morning tends to color one's activities through the day. A person on arising may proclaim "I am nothing but a bit of scum on an accidental little world whirling in a blind universe." Another faces the world with the thought that life is a great privilege and a divine gift. One starts with the idea that he is a blind pawn in a meaningless, purposeless world. The other feels that he is endowed with an immortal soul and that he will be held responsible for his actions. One maintains that life is aimless; the other asserts that man is the captain of his destiny and that he must chart his own course. Which of the two persons is more likely to give a good moral account of his day's activities? The practices of the first may be better than his protestations. The second may fail to apply his ideal to his practices. But the moral odds are definitely in favor of the second who starts the day as a candidate for the good life.

2. *A sacred trust*

The traditional Jew starts the day with the following thoughts:

I must not take life for granted. It is a sacred trust. What am I doing with it?

I am not a beast. I am endowed with a soul, i.e., with the power of conscious, creative, spiritual growth. How have I grown? What have I created?

It is difficult for me to stand on my own feet. I cannot grow fully in isolation. I need the Torah, the wisdom and experience of Israel, and I need a proper environment and the companionship of good men. How do I meet these needs?

My standard of behavior must be not only the approval of my neighbor but my own conscience and my self-respect.

I must express my ideals concretely in worthy acts and in the service of communal institutions.

Of these thoughts the Jew is daily reminded by the traditional Morning Prayers:

"I give thanks unto Thee, O King Who liveth and endureth, Who hast mercifully restored my soul unto me; great is Thy faithfulness." [1]

"O my God, the soul which Thou gavest me is pure; Thou didst create it, Thou didst form it, Thou didst breathe it unto me; Thou preservest it within me; and wilt take it from me, but wilt restore it unto me hereafter." [2]

"May it be Thy will, O Lord our God and God of our fathers, to make us familiar with Thy law, and make us cleave to Thy commandments. O lead us not into the power of sin or of transgression or of iniquity or of temptation or of scorn. Let not the evil inclination have sway over us. Keep us from an evil man and an evil companion. Make us cleave to the good inclination and to good works." [3]

"At all times let a man fear God as well in private as in public, acknowledge the truth, and speak the truth in his heart." [4]

3. A moral pattern

As a suggestive pattern for permanent values the following Mishna is recited:

"These are the things the fruit of which a man enjoys in this world, while the stock remains for him in the world to come: viz., honoring father and mother, the practice of charity, timely attendance at the house of study morning and evening, hospitality to wayfarers, visiting the sick, dowering the bride, attending the dead at the grave, devotion in prayer, and making peace between man and his neighbor, and the study of the Torah balances them all." [5]

Is not a person who starts the day with such a deep sense of moral responsibility and with an expressed will for ethical conduct and for socially constructive action, more likely to act fairly and decently than the person whose morning thoughts are only of physical needs and material gains?

Questions for Discussion

1. How would you define "soul"?
2. Which Jewish institution or organization today offers the best environment for Jewish growth and creativity?

3. What is meant by "evil inclination"? By what standards do we evaluate companions as good or evil?
4. Are all the practices and institutions mentioned in the Mishna cited essential today? What are some of their modern equivalents?

CHAPTER II

God

1. Not a philosophic abstraction

To the Jew, God is not a philosophic abstraction. He is the Creator. "In the beginning God created the heavens and the earth" (Gen. 1:1). He is the *Ribbono Shel Olam,* "The Master of the Universe." But He is more than that. He is the essence of all morality and righteousness. He is the supreme ideal of moral conduct. Man is to pattern his conduct after the attributes of the Divine.

Jewish philosophers from time to time did philosophize about the existence of God. But it was more in response to the intellectual fashion of their day than to the inner need of the Jewish philosopher. It was to show the Gentile philosopher, or the untraditional Jew who is inclined to accept philosophic reasoning as the final authority on truth, that the Jewish concept of God is in accord with the best philosophies of the day. But to the traditional Jew himself God is not the result of reasoning but the very essence of life which he felt even as he felt all the needs of life.

To the Jew only "the fool sayeth in his heart there is no God," [1] even as the blind man may insist that there is no such thing as color. But the man with vision sees colors; he need not argue about their existence. Even so the Jew saw God. He saw God in nature and in human nature; he saw God in the world of matter and he saw God in the world of men—in history.

2. God in Nature

The Jew sees God in nature:

> The heavens proclaim God's splendor,
> the sky speaks of His handiwork;

4

day after day takes up the tale,
night after night makes Him known;
their speech has never a word,
not a souud for the ear,
yet their message spreads
the wide world over,
their meaning carries
to earth's end.[2]

In a similar manner the rabbis described their experience of God: When Pharaoh asked Moses and Aaron, "Who is your God that I should hearken unto His voice?" they replied: "The universe is filled with the might and power of our God. He existed ere the world was created, and He will continue to exist when the world comes to an end. He formed you and infused you with the breath of life. He stretched forth the heaven and laid the foundations of the earth. . . . He makes the rains and dew to descend, and causes the herbage to sprout. He also forms the embryo in the mother's womb and enables it to issue forth as a living being."[3]

Observing the regular sequence of day and night and the change of the seasons, the Jew, unlike the pagans around him, conceived them not as wilful expressions of different deities but as the manifestations of One Universal God, the Designer of the laws of nature. As day changes into night the Jew prays:

"Blessed art Thou, O Lord our God, King of the universe, Who at Thy word bringest on the evening twilight, with wisdom openest the gates of heavens, and with understanding changest times and variest seasons, and arrangest the stars according to Thy will. Thou createst day and night; Thou rollest away the light before the darkness and darkness before the light."[4]

Throughout the universe, in all the forces of nature, in the mineral and vegetable worlds, in the instincts of beasts and in the efforts of man, the Jew sees God: "Bless the Lord, O my soul. . . . He covereth Himself with light as with a garment; He stretcheth out the heavens like a curtain. . . . He maketh winds His messengers; His ministers, flaming fire. . . . He sendeth forth springs into the valleys; they run among the mountains. They give drink to every beast of the plain. . . . By them the birds of heaven have their dwelling, they utter their voice from among the branches. . . . He causeth grass to grow for the cattle, and herbs for the service of man, that he may bring forth bread from the earth . . . . Thou makest darkness and it is night; therein all the beasts of the forest do move. The sun arises, they get away to lie down in their dens. Man goeth forth unto his work and his labor until the evening. How manifold are Thy works. O Lord! In wisdom hast Thou made them all; the earth is full of Thy possessions." [5]

3. The divine unity

Seeing nature as the work of a divine unity, of a universal God of justice and righteousness, the Jew does not face the world of nature with fear and trembling. It is not a world of chaos. It is a world upon which one may depend. It is a world moving by divine laws. It is a world which is not intrinsically hostile to man; it is a world which can be trusted, and within the framework of which man can plan and organize his moral life. The Jew, therefore, early in his history gave up the pagan belief in the need to appease the spirits of the various and wilful forces of nature and to placate the demons assumed to be lurking everywhere to trap the children of man. (At most, such tendencies played but a minor role in authoritative Judaism.) The Jew conceives man and the world around him as products of the same divine spirit. Living according to the divine will, man therefore finds nature not a wilful foe but a trusted ally, gradually yielding to man's growing wisdom its substance, its sustenance and its secrets. "So God formed man . . . male and female he formed both. And God blessed them; God said to them: 'Be fruitful and multiply, fill the earth and subdue it, mastering the fish of the sea, the birds of the air, and every living creature that crawls on earth'" (Gen. 2:27–28). .

The process of creation, however, has not reached its final form and objective. God continues to reveal Himself in the eternally creative and recreative laws of nature. "He in His goodness reneweth the creation every day continually." [6]

4. God in man

Some of the natural phenomena are left as raw material to be shaped by man who, created in the image of God, is thus endowed with the power of being a *Shutaf Le'maase V'reshit,* a "co-creator" with God.

Just as God is revealed in nature, so He is revealed in human nature. He manifests Himself in the infinite universe and in the human microcosm.

God reveals Himself in man only when man expresses the will of God, when he is just and creative. When man violates the laws of justice and creativity, he obscures the divine presence and mars the divine plan. God limited Himself to give man the freedom to choose his conduct. He endowed man with the power and freedom to choose whether to follow the divine will or not. "Everything is in the power of Heaven except (man's) fear of Heaven." [7]

Man is free to choose but he is not free to avoid the consequences of his choice. "For I have put before you this day life and welfare, death and misfortune. . . . Here and now I call heaven and earth to witness against you that I have put life and death before you, the blessing and the curse; choose life, then, that you and your children may live, by loving the Eternal your God, obeying His voice, and holding fast to Him, for that means life to you and length of days." [8]

5. Divine attributes

It is by imitating God's attributes that man is true to his nature as a being created in the image of God. What are the divine attributes? Scripture replies: "The Lord, the Lord, merciful and gracious, slow to anger and abounding in loving-kindness and truth; keeping mercy unto the thousandth generation, forgetting iniquity and transgression and sin, and acquitting the penitent." [9]

How then can man imitate Him? Even as He is merciful and gracious, man, too, must be merciful and gracious. But mercy must not degenerate into extreme sentimentalism which may undermine law and justice. "Said the Holy One, blessed be He: 'If I create the world with the attribute of mercy, sins will multiply beyond all bounds; if I create it only with the attribute of law, how can the world last! Behold, I will create it with both attributes; would that it might endure.'" [10] Not blind justice but justice tempered with mercy is the ideal.

6. *Witnessing God's presence*

When man executes justice for the fatherless and the widow and loves the stranger, he testifies to the presence of God.[11] Conversely, "He that oppresseth the poor blasphemeth his Maker." [12] There are four classes of people who do not experience the divine presence: scoffers, liars, hypocrites and slanderers.[13]

Said the Rabbis: "Who are God's friends? Those who, being persecuted, do not persecute in return; those who hearing themselves offended are patiently silent; those who act from purest motives, doing good from love of God; those who accept cheerfully the chastening rod." [14]

On the other hand, "Who is the most hateful person? He who denies his Creator. It is this denial which leads a man to unsocial and vicious practices. Honor thy father and mother, thou shalt not commit adultery, thou shalt not covet—behold, a person does not repudiate any of these laws until he repudiates the root of them, and nobody proceeds to commit a transgression without first having denied Him Who prohibited it." [15]

7. *The Fatherhood of God*

The Fatherhood of God is identified with the free expression of the Brotherhood of Man: "He who rejoices on the festivals but does not give to the Holy One, blessed be He, His due share,is selfish. . . . To give a portion to the Holy One, blessed be He, means to make glad the poor according to one's ability. For on those days He goes to look at those broken vessels of His. He comes to them, and, seeing that they have nothing with which to rejoice on the festival, He weeps over them." [16]

Questions for Discussion

1. What are the moral implications in viewing God merely as the First Cause or conceiving Him as the Judge of the Universe?

2. What are the social implications in the concept, "Man is created in the image of God?" Can this concept be reconciled with the Aryan or similar racial theories? Is it in conflict with the idea of the "Chosen People"?
3. Contrast the Jewish concept of God as tempering justice with mercy and the classic concept of justice symbolized by a Blind Goddess.
4. Can superstition and tatoos be reconciled with the concept of God throughout nature?
5. What are the implications of the Fatherhood of God in regard to international relations, immigration restrictions, standards in philanthropic institutions?

CHAPTER III

The Problem of Evil

1. Suffering of the innocent

In a polytheistic or dualistic conception of the world the existence of evil offers no moral problem. Evil is assumed to be the work of a deity over whom the just God has no control. But once you accept the belief that the universe is ruled by one God whose attributes are justice and righteousness there arises the challenging questions: How do you explain the existence of evil in the world? How do you account for so much pain and suffering? Why is Israel persecuted? Why do the innocent suffer?

2. Man's limited view

These questions are not new. The problem is implied in the earliest book of the Bible, in Abraham's plea: "Wilt Thou consume the righteous with the wicked? . . . Shall not the judge of all the earth do right?" (Gen. 18:23-25). According to the rabbis, this was the problem which Moses tried to solve when he asked: "If I have found favor with Thee, pray let me understand Thy ways with men, that I may understand Thy nature. . . . Let me see Thy majesty." But the Eternal replied: "You cannot see my full face, for no man can live after seeing me. . . . But there is a spot near me, where you place yourself on the rocks; and when my majesty sweeps by, I will put you into a cleft, covering you with my hand till I sweep past you; then I will remove my hand, to let you see my back. My face is never to be seen." [1] In other words, man's life is too short to comprehend the divine plan. Looking back in history he may get a glimpse of the progressive pattern but the full purpose and design man cannot grasp.

3. Job

This is the problem dramatized in the Book of Job. Why does God permit the innocent to suffer, is Job's persistent plaint: "He destroys blameless and bad men alike. He does not? Well, who is it then? When He is scourging us with sudden death, He mocks at the despair of innocent men. The world is handed over to the wicked; He makes the rulers of men blind to justice." [2]

What is the answer given to Job? "Listen to this, O Job, stand still, think of the wonders of God. When God works, do you know how? How He makes lightning flash from the clouds? . . . How can we argue with our darkened minds? . . . The Almighty is beyond our minds. Supreme in power and rich in justice, He violates no right." [3] Just as we do not understand God's wonders in nature, we do not understand God's purpose for man. Not knowing the ultimate purpose we cannot know what is good or bad for us. What may appear evil for the moment may prove to be good when the whole plan is revealed.

4. Jeremiah's faith

Jeremiah was perplexed by the problem of the apparent success of the evil doers: "Thou art always in the right, Eternal One, when I complain to Thee; yet I would argue this with Thee— Why do bad men prosper? Why are scoundrels secure and serene? Thou plantest them and they take root, they flourish, yes and they bear fruit." [4] But his faith rose above his doubts, and he spent his life pleading with his people not to be tempted by the allurements of pagan associations but to remain loyal to the ideals of their fathers and to seek security not in pagan alliances but in a God of justice and righteousness. If Israel survived through the centuries it is because there was a saving-remnant which shared Jeremiah's faith.

5. The Psalmist

To the Psalmist the apparent prosperity of the wicked is the bait leading to his destruction, the pride which comes before a fall:

I almost slipped,
I nearly lost my footing,
In 'anger at the godless and their arrogance,
    At the sight of their success. . . .
    So people turn to follow them,
    Thinking, 'What does God care?
    How can the Almighty heed—
    When these, the godless prosperously fare,
    Thriving thus at their ease?' . . .
    Sorely it troubled me,
    Till I found out God's secret,
    Viewing their latter end.
    Thou plantest them on slippery ground. . . .[5]

6. *Evil result of misdirected freedom*

The medieval Jewish philosopher explains the existence of evil not as something which is intrinsically bad in anything which God created but rather as something which results from the freedom and power with which God endowed man to control and make use of the world of nature. It is man's abuse of his freedom and of the laws of nature that causes much of the evil in the world.

"Just as God created all things with certain qualities, man, for example, with the faculty of speech, and as He created things incapable of certain qualities (as the stone is forever wordless)—in the same way He created certain things which He endowed with the possibility of acquiring certain qualities. . . . God has made a certain object indeterminate, and has created it in such a way that it may equally acquire one of two opposite qualities . . . For if it were affirmed that all events depend, like the eclipses of the moon, upon natural laws, and are either inevitable or impossible, and if it were affirmed that God has left no latitude with regard to that which decides the being or not being of each phenomenon—and if this contention were so, then the world would be ruined, society destroyed and even eternal life without hope. In vain would man labor, build houses, plant trees, tame the wild beasts, forge sword or lance for combat—for everything would be predetermined; and in vain would he be pious, since either his piety or his impiety would have been determined in advance—all of which is in obvious contradiction to the truth. God, of set purpose, created the possible, as possible, and He knows with absolute precision the subjectively possible which is objectively inevitable. For there are things that happen to man which are not always desired of God, but there are certain things which make clear the divine intent, for they follow from natural causes, and are either harmful or beneficial according to whether the man put nature to a wrong or right use." [6]

A similar view is expressed by Maimonides: "The numerous evils to which individuals are exposed are due to the defects existing in the persons themselves. We complain and seek relief from our own faults: we suffer from evils which we, by our own free will, inflict on ourselves and ascribe them to God. . . . The evils that befall man are of three kinds:

a. "The first kind of evil is that which is caused man by the circumstance that . . . he possesses a body. It is on account of the body that some persons happen to have great deformities or paralysis of some of the organs. . . . But genesis can only take place through destruction. . . . He who thinks that he can have flesh and bones without being subject to any external influence, or any of the accidents of matter, unconsciously wishes to reconcile two opposites, viz., to be at the same time subject and not subject to change. If man were never subject to change there would be no generation. . . . You will, nevertheless, find that the evils of the above are rare . . . deformed individuals are few in number.

b. "The second class of evils are those which people cause to each other. . . . These are not frequent if the whole inhabited part of the world is taken into consideration.

c. "The third class of evils are those which man causes by his own actions. This is the largest class. . . . It is especially of these evils that most men complain. . . . This class of evils originates in man's excessive desire to indulgence (which) brings diseases and affliction upon the body and soul alike. . . . For desire is without limit, whilst the things which are necessary are few in number. . . . Those who are perverse in their thoughts are constantly in trouble. . . . They expose themselves to great troubles for the purpose of obtaining that which is not necessary. When they meet with the consequences of the course which

they adopt, they complain of the decrees and judgments of God. . . .
Observe how nature proves the correctness of this assertion. The more
necessary a thing is for living beings, the more easily it is to be found
and the cheaper it is; the less necessary it is, the rarer and dearer it is.
. . . It is no wrong or injustice . . . that one has not those things which
are not necessary; he who has them has only something illusory or
deceptive." [7]

7. Moral warning and test

Viewing life on earth as but a fraction of life eternal, the rabbis often
accepted suffering as a timely and loving Providential warning to take
stock of one's moral conduct so as to be worthy of the higher and enduring happiness: "Let a man rejoice in suffering more than in happiness;
for a man who has lived all his life in happiness, any sin which he may
have committed has not been pardoned . . . but sufferings secure ac-
ceptance." [8]

Suffering may be a moral challenge and a spiritual test. It may be a
divine compliment paid to a strong character: "Should a man see suffering come upon him, let him scrutinize his actions. . . . If he can thus
find no cause, it is certain that his sufferings are chastenings of love." [9]
"Why should suffering be inflicted upon the righteous? The answer is,
'The potter does not test cracked vessels, for he need only knock upon
them once and they break; but he tests sound vessels.'" [10]

8. Humanity is one

Conceiving humanity as one, Judaism regards the suffering of the
righteous as an atonement for the sins of the world: "When the righteous
are afflicted by illness or sufferings . . . it is that all the sinners of their
generation may receive redemption. We can see a similar process in
the human body. At the time when all the members of the human
body suffer through an illness, then one member must be operated
upon, so that all the remaining members may recover. . . . So it is with
the children of the world, its members are to each other, like members
of the human body each to the other. At the time the Holy One,
blessed be He, desires to give health (sanctification) to the world,

He afflicts a just person with sickness and pain and, through him, gives health to the world." [11]

9. *No proof of sin*

Certainly the fact that an individual or a people suffers is no proof that the sufferer is more sinful than others and is rejected by God. On this point all Jewish thinkers are in agreement with the author of the Book of Job. Conversely, temporary success and prosperity are no indication of the righteousness of the successful:

"I see thee reproaching us with our degradation and poverty, but the best of other religions boast of both. Do they not glorify him who said: 'He who smites thee on the right cheek, turn to him the left also.' . . . He and his friends and followers, after hundreds of years of contumely, flogging and slaying, attained their well-known success, and just in these things they glory. This is also the history of the founder of Islam and his friends, who eventually prevailed, and became powerful. The nations boast of these, but not of kings whose power and might are great, whose walls are strong, and whose chariots are terrifying. . . . If we bear our exile and degradation for God's sake, as is meet, we shall be the pride of the generation which will come with the Messiah." [12]

"The proof they bring from the prosperity of those who believe in their faith is no proof at all. . . . Surely the fact that Sennacherib and Nebuchadnezzar and Alexander were successful over Israel is no sign that their faith was better than that of Israel. Even now the Christians maintain that the law of the Mohammedans is positive and conventional, not divine, and yet they are successful and rule over a great part of the world. It seems clear therefore that the prosperity of a nation is no proof of the truth of its faith." [13]

10. *Ultimate justice*

In general the Jew accepts the hardships of life in a spirit of humble faith in the ultimate justice of God. Suffering a great loss, he recites with Job: "The Lord hath given, the Lord hath taken, blessed be the name of the Lord." In case of a death the mourners recite the traditional Kaddish, which begins with the words, "Magnified and sanctified be

His great name in the world which He created according to His will." It is all a manifestation of His infinite, incomprehensible will. Somehow, somewhere, in God's own time we may gain a deeper insight into His plan and we may understand the purpose of our suffering.

11. Accepting life's terms

But while we do not understand and do not have the power fully to determine our lot, it is in our power to determine our reaction to it. "According to ancient Jewish custom, the ceremony of cutting our garments when our nearest and dearest on earth is lying dead before us, is to be performed *standing up.* This teaches us to meet all sorrow standing upright. The future may be dark, veiled from the eye of mortals—but not the manner in which we are to meet the future. To rail at life, to rebel against a destiny that has cast our lines in unpleasant places, is of no avail. We cannot lay down terms to life. Life must be accepted on its own terms. But hard as life's terms are, life (it has been finely said) never dictates unrighteousness, unholiness, dishonor." [14]

Questions for Discussion

1. How does the author of Job present the problem of evil? What is his answer?
2. What are the greatest evils of our day? Can man blame God for these evils?
3. To what extent is the wide-spread rejection of the implications of the Unity of God and the Unity of Man responsible for the chief evils of our day?
4. Can the evils of disease and poverty be checked if man were to give to such efforts the energy now given to class struggle, international wars and rivalry?

CHAPTER IV

Man

1. In, but not of, the Animal Kingdom

The most fundamental Jewish thought regarding man is that man is not a beast; he is not just another species of animal. Like other animals his body is earthly, but he is endowed with a spirit which reaches out toward heaven. He reflects the image of God. This is the basic principle upon which Judaism—upon which all Torah, all responsible human life—is posited. "Which is the basic principle of the Torah? The verse in Genesis 5:1, 'This is the book of the generations of man. . . . In the image of God created He him.' " [1]

Hence human life is sacred. No property rights can compare with human rights. "One human being is worth the whole of creation." [2] Individual personality is invaluable. "Man was first created as a single individual to teach the lesson that whoever destroys one human life, Scripture marks him as if he had destroyed the whole world." [3]

Man is in the animal kingdom but not of the animal kingdom. "In four respects man resembles the beings above and in four respects he is like the animals below. Like the animals he eats and drinks, propagates his species, relieves himself, and dies. Like the ministering angels he stands erect, speaks, possesses intellect, and can look upward." [4] Man can look upward and forward. All other animals live in two dimensions of time. They live in the present and have memories of the past. Man lives in the present, can preserve the memories of the past and can consciously plan the future. He lives in three dimensions of time.

2. Climax of creation

Man is the climax of creation. More than that, man is to continue the process of creation; he is to be a *Shutaf le'maase v'reshit,* a co-creator with God.

"We must not say that the animal species are more perfect in their organization than man because they require no shade or shelter from the heat or storm, nor preparation of the food they need, which nature provides ready for their use. . . . Similarly they do not have to prepare weapons with which to fight against their enemies, for they are provided with natural weapons. . . . Nor do they need to make themselves any garments . . . whereas man is devoid of all these things. . . .

"If we consider the various forms, we find that they follow an ascending series in regard to quality. The latter form is superior to the prior one, as though matter in receiving form proceeds from imperfection to perfection . . . gradually ascending from an inferior grade of existence to a more perfect one. Thus matter first receives the forms of the elements, then it rises to the stage of minerals . . . then it attains to the grade of plants . . . animals . . . man. . . . Here the process comes to an end. . . .

"Man is nobler and more perfect than all, since in him are combined all the earlier forms. . . . He has the power of comprehending the general, whereas the lower animals perceive only the particular, having no power to comprehend the universal." [5]

3. Conscious of self

Not only is he different from the other animals but he is conscious of that difference. In this very consciousness lies his greatest distinction and his greatest divine privilege. Said Rabbi Akiba: "Beloved is man in that he was created in the image of God; greater love was shown to him in that he was made conscious that he was created in the image of God." [6]

But this awareness of his creative abilities and his superior powers must be accompanied by responsibility. Man is therefore held accountable for all his actions. "Reflect upon three things, and thou wilt not come within the power of sin: know what is above thee—a seeing eye, a hearing ear, and all thy deeds written in a book." [7]

4. Self-discipline

The first act of responsibility is self-discipline which is far from an easy task. "Who is mighty? He who controls his passions." [8] Self-discipline is a slow and continuous process. "He who trains himself in (God's) service should not begin with difficult tasks but with lighter ones, and if he cannot do all, he should do as much as he can. And he should progressively assume more and more responsibilities. . . . Passion is at all times waging war against reason. . . . Man has the power to choose which of these contending forces he is to support." [9]

"The pious man is nothing but a prince who is obeyed by his senses and by his mental as well as his physical faculties, which he governs. . . . He is fit to rule, because if he were the prince of a country he would be as just as he is to his body and soul. He subdues his passions, keeping them in bonds, and at the same time giving them their share in order to satisfy them as regards food, drink, cleanliness, and so forth. . . . If then he has satisfied each of them, he calls upon his community as a respected prince calls upon his disciplined army, to assist him in reaching the divine degree." [10]

5. The golden mean

In this process of self-control, not extreme abstinence but the Golden Mean is the Jewish ideal. "An individual is not permitted to indulge in too many fast-days." [11] "One will have to explain to the Creator for having failed to enjoy the food which he was given to enjoy." [12]

The following legend illustrates the historic Jewish attitude toward intoxicating drinks. "When Noah planted the vine, Satan offered his cooperation which was accepted. Thereupon Satan poured over the plant the blood of a lamb, a lion, a monkey and a swine. He thus taught Noah that when a man takes one drink of wine, he is humble like a lamb. When he takes another drink, he becomes as bold and arrogant as a lion. Another drink, and he begins to act like a monkey. More drinks, and he wallows in the gutter like a swine!" [13]

"The divine law imposes no asceticism on us. It rather desires that we should keep the middle path, and grant every mental and physical faculty its due without overburdening one faculty at the expense of another. . . . Prolonged fasting is no act of piety for a weak person. . . . Neither is diminution of wealth an act of piety, if the wealth is gained in a lawful way, and if its acquisition does not interfere with study and good works." [14]

6. Humility

The trait which is most conducive to the necessary self-discipline is humility. Judaism exalts humility as one of the prime virtues, the *sine qua non* of nearly all other virtues. "Whoever is humble causes the *Shekinah* to dwell with man on earth." [15] "Every man who is filled with an arrogant spirit is as though he had worshipped idols, denied the basic principles of religion, and committed every kind of immorality." [16] "A good eye (i.e. an un-envious disposition), a humble mind, and a lowly spirit are attributes of the disciples of Abraham our father." [17] The rabbis who constantly held up the ideal of scholarship found it necessary to warn against the arrogance of scholarship. "If a man makes himself like a wilderness upon which all may tread, his learning will endure in him, otherwise it will not." [18] Meekness is one of the forty-eight qualifications requisite in a student of the Torah.[19]

Since a wise man is he who learns from everyone, one must "be humble before every person." Humility is an ingredient which must come with all other virtues. "Just as a house is incomplete without the humble door-step (upon which all tread), so is a person, regardless of all virtues, incomplete without humility." [20]

While youth should be humble before the aged, age in itself is no cause for pride and arrogance. Said the rabbis: "Why was man created last of all creatures? So that if man becomes too arrogant, even an insect may tell him that it arrived first." [21] When individuals or groups boast of their superiority simply because they belong to the "old families" or to the "original settlers," the retort may well be made: "The insects came there at an earlier date." The mere fact of having been in the place earlier or longer is not necessarily proof of superiority or of worthy accomplishments.

Questions for Discussion

1. Make a list of traits wherein man differs from other animals.
2. Discuss some traditional Jewish customs which make for personal and group discipline.
3. What is the Jewish attitude toward the Prohibition movement?
4. What is the Jewish evaluation of the slogan, "America for Americans"?
5. Does the concept of the "Chosen People" violate the virtue of humility?

CHAPTER V

Mercy

1. The quality of mercy

Mercy is one of the qualities which raise man above the animal level. It is one of the divine attributes which man is to express in his life. "How can man resemble God? Even as He is gracious and merciful, be thou gracious and merciful." [1] Mercy brings man nearer to God. "Seven qualities avail before the Throne of Glory: faith, righteousness, justice, loving-kindness, mercy, truth and peace." [2]

No one is so poor but that he can exercise the quality of mercy. Said a sage of old: "Help every man cheerfully. If you have not the means to provide what the person needs, show him at least your profound sympathy. I know I often walked for miles with an unfortunate person and wept with him when I could not help him otherwise." [3]

2. No class restrictions

Mercy must not be limited to one's group or class. This is illustrated by the following popular dictum: Among the unclean birds enumerated in Leviticus XI, there is the *Hasidah* (stork). The Hebrew term, *Hasidah,* literally means the "Pious One." The rabbis explain that the bird is called the Pious One because she shows loving-kindness to her associates. The question is then raised: "If so, why is the bird classed among the unclean?" And the reply is: "Because she shows loving-kindness *only* to her associates." No matter how pious one may appear, if one limits one's mercy and kindliness to one's own group or class, he is "Shekez," an "abomination."

3. Even to enemies

Nay, one must extend the quality of mercy even to one's enemies. It may be necessary to punish those who wronged us, but one must not rejoice at their suffering. "When the Egyptians were drowning in the sea the angels wanted to sing songs of exaltation, but the Holy One, blessed be He, disapproved, saying: 'The work of my hands are drowning in the sea, and you are singing!' " [4]

The same thought is expressed in a quaint custom of the Passover Eve Seder ritual. When the Jew recites the story of the plagues suffered by the Egyptians, he pours out from his cup of wine a drop for each plague. For the Jew does not consider his "Cup of Salvation" complete when it comes through the suffering of any of God's children. Hence the more plagues the Egyptians suffered, the less full is the Jewish cup and the less complete his happiness. [5]

4. Cruelty to animals

One must be merciful even to dumb creatures. *Zaar Baale Haim*, the prevention of cruelty to animals, is one of the historic ideals of Judaism. Many of the laws of *Shehita*, the traditional form of slaughtering animals, are motivated by the desire to reduce the pain of the animal.

One is not permitted to buy an animal unless he has provided food for it. [6] One may not eat in the morning before he has fed the livestock. [7] There is a legend that Rabbi Judah HaNasi was punished with sickness because he showed no compassion for a calf; he was cured when he showed consideration for kittens. [8]

Questions for Discussion

1. What were the Greek and Roman attitudes toward *Zaar Baale Haim?* What is our modern attitude as revealed in such organizations as the Society for the Prevention of Cruelty to Animals?
2. How does *Shehita* reduce the suffering of the animal?
3. Are mercy and law incompatible? Is mercy compatible with justice?
4. Is the probation office in American courts a result of Roman law or of Jewish thought in the Judeo-Christian tradition?
5. What should be the Jewish attitude toward Prize Fights?

CHAPTER VI

Faith

1. The basic virtue

Faith is the essence of all other virtues. Said the rabbis: "Six hundred and thirteen commandments were addressed to Moses—365 prohibitions corresponding to the number of days in the solar year, and 248 positive commands corresponding to the number of limbs in the human body. David came and reduced them to eleven principles, which are enumerated in the fifteenth psalm: 'Lord, who may sojourn in Thy tent and who may dwell on Thy holy mount? He that walketh uprightly, and worketh righteousness, and speaketh the truth in his heart; that uttereth no calumny with his tongue, that doeth no evil to his neighbor; and bringeth no reproach to his fellowman; in whose eyes the despicable is despised; but that honoureth those who fear the Lord; that sweareth to his own injury and changeth not; that putteth not out his money for usury, and taketh no bribe against the innocent.'

"Isaiah came and reduced them to six: 'He that walketh righteously and speaketh uprightly, he that despises the gain of oppression, that withholds his hands from bribes, that would listen to no plans of murder and shutteth his eyes from looking at evil' (Is. 33:15).

"Micah came and reduced them to three: 'What doth the Lord require of thee, but to do justly and to love mercy and to walk humbly with thy God' (Micah 6:8). . . . . Lastly came Habakkuk and reduced them to one: 'The righteous shall live by their faith.' " [1]

2. Rabbinic examples

There are many interesting rabbinic examples of men of faith or the lack thereof. "Whoever has a morsel of bread in his basket and says,

'What shall I eat tomorrow?' belongs to those who are of small faith." [2]

There was Nahum, the man of Gamzo. Why was he called *Gamzo?* Because whatever happened to him, he used to exclaim, "gam zo le-tovah," "This also is for good." [3] Rabbi Akiba too used to say, "What-ever the All-merciful does, He does for the best." Once Rabbi Akiba was refused hospitality at a certain town. So he said, "Whatever the All-merciful does is for the best." He spent the night in a field. He had with him a cock, an ass, and a lamp. A gust of wind came and extinguished the lamp, a cat came and ate up the cock, and a lion came and devoured the ass. Rabbi Akiba remarked, "Whatever the All-merciful does is for the best." That night a band of robbers came and plundered the town. Rabbi Akiba then told the inhabitants, "Did I not tell you whatever the Holy One, blessed be He, does is all for the best!" [4]

3. Not blind faith

The Jewish ideal of faith does not imply sitting with folded hands waiting for miracles, or deliberately violating the laws of nature, con-fident of a miracle. In fact the rabbis warned against such blind faith. "One must not wait for a miracle." [5] "Everything is in the power of Heaven except sickness from cold droughts (which is man's own fault)." [6]

4. Hassidic dicta

Hassidic literature lays much stress on the ideal of faith. Among the dicta of the Bratzlaver Rabbi we find: "False trust is the belief that God will bless dishonest deeds and protect the transgressor from dis-covery. False trust is the belief that God will grant a man success, even if he expands beyond his financial means and borrows heedlessly from other people."

"Redemption depends on faith; lack of faith was the cause of our exile. To attain faith concentrate the full power of the mind upon the words of your prayer.

"When our faith is weak, the Lord denies us a true leader.

"All virtues rest on the foundation of faith in God.

"A man must not rely upon pure reason; he must mix faith with it.

"Unworthy teachings bring unbelief and enmity to religion; knowledge is imperfect without faith.

"When faith is weakened, opportunities for a peaceful livelihood are missing; men do not aid each other.

"Faith is the portal to holiness. . . . Faith expands within a man, and gives him patience, joy and diligence. Such faith is easiest to acquire in *Eretz Yisroel.*

"Faith should not only rest in the heart; it should also be expressed by word of mouth. The utterance of words of faith strengthens a man's faith." [7]

Only the life of a man of faith may be called true living. "A man of faith has confidence and never descends to despair." [8]

How is faith generated? Where does one find the necessary faith?

"Humility and study of the Torah lead to faith. . . . When doubt of the Lord's decrees comes to your mind, keep silent. Your own thoughts will then answer you. . . . Envy, anger and pride cause loss of faith." [9]

Faith is the basis for worship. "There can be service of the Lord from tradition without learning. But there can be no service of the Lord without faith." [10]

5. Faith and reason

Faith transcends but does not reject man's mental efforts to understand the world. "Every man should discipline his mind. He should study and reflect to the utmost of his ability. When he has reached a point where he is unable to comprehend further, he may submit to faith, and return to the learning within his grasp. Beyond a certain degree of research, both the sage and the ignorant man are alike." [11]

Faith respects the findings of the scientists but is aware of their limitations. Man's latest answer to any problem is not necessarily the final one. The following ancedote shows the Jewish attitude concerning the relationship between science and faith:

A famous physician examined a rabbi and told the family that the patient could not survive. They were naturally shocked. Noting their grief and suspecting the cause, the rabbi told them: "The Talmud points out that the Bible (Ex. 21:19) authorizes a physician to heal. He may therefore prescribe for life, but he has no divine authority to prescribe death. There is still the Great Healer!" [12]

Questions for Discussion

1. What is the difference between faith and superstition?
2. Discuss the philosophy of "Gam zo le-tovah." When is it helpful and under what conditions is it harmful?
3. What is the Jewish attitude toward "Salvation by Faith" and "Salvation by Works"?
4. What is the proper relationship between faith and action?

CHAPTER VII

Prayer

1. Not all petition

Prayer is worship of the heart. It is the soul's speech to God, and it takes different forms to match the various emotions it would express. When it gives utterance to our hopes and our needs, it takes the form of petition and supplication. But all prayer is not petition. Sometimes the memory of blessings, rather than the desire for them, fills the heart to overflowing, and moves us to commune with God and offer thanks. We thank Him for His mercies shown to us or to the world at large. Or we express our adoration for the wonders of the universe.[1]

Of all the various kinds of prayer those are the highest which ask for nothing—nothing, at least for ourselves. Even the prayers for ourselves should be less about worldly than about spiritual things. The traditional Jewish prayers ask sparingly for material benefits but stress the higher blessings—courage under affliction, strength under temptation, guidance in life's complexities.[2]

2. Mood for prayer

Prayer requires the proper mood, the power of concentration and a spirit of humility. "When thou prayest regard not thy prayer as a fixed mechanical task, but as an appeal for mercy and grace before the All-present." [3] "When you pray, know before whom you stand." [4] In proper devotion a man has his eyes downward and his heart upward.[5] Prayer without devotion is like a body without a soul.[6]

One must pray with clean hands and a pure heart. "The prayers of the man whose hands are tainted are not answered, for his supplication is turbid, being under transgression. Therefore man is bound to cleanse his heart (from every covetousness) before he prays." [7]

The Jewish mystics laid great stress on prayer. "Prayer is spiritual worship. Deep mysteries are attached to it, for a man can hardly conceive how his prayer cleaves the eternal spaces, cleaves the firmament, opens doors and ascends on high. . . . It behooves, then, every man, after equipping himself with the emblems of holiness (*Tallith* and *Tefillin*), to attune his heart and his inner being for the act of worship and to say his prayers with devotion. For the words that he utters ascend on high, for the scrutiny of angelic supervisors. . . . If the prayer be uttered fitly, he (the angelic supervisor) with the other chieftains, kisses that utterance and carries it aloft. . . . Then the letters of the divine Name that abide in the ethereal spaces soar upwards . . . with the prayer." [8]

3. The Shema

The *Shema* is the heart of the traditional Jewish prayer. "Hear, O Israel, the Lord is our God, the Lord is One!" That is at once the quintessential embodiment of all our philosophy, as well as chief among Israel's contributions to the everlasting truths of religion. The first prayer of innocent child-lips, the last confession of the dying, *Shema* has been the watchword and the rallying-cry of a hundred generations in Israel. By it they were welded into one Brotherhood to do the will of their Father who is in Heaven. The reading of the *Shema* has—in rabbinic phrase—clothed Israel with invincible lion-strength, and endowed him with the double-edged sword of the spirit against the unutterable terrors of his long night in exile. [9]

The *Shema* is recited upon rising in the morning and upon retiring at night. The Jew has it inscribed in the *Tefillin* which he places on his arm and on his head, and it is attached to his doorpost (*Mezuzah*). It stresses the unity of God, and the duty of continuous study:

"Hear, O Israel, the Lord is our God, the Lord is One. And thou shalt love the Lord thy God with all thy heart, and with all thy soul, and with all thy might. And these words, which I command thee this day, shall be upon thy heart; and thou shalt teach them diligently unto thy children, and shalt talk of them when thou sittest in thy house, and when thou walkest by the way, and when thou liest down and when thou risest up. And thou shalt bind them for a sign upon thy hand, and they shall be for frontlets between thine eyes. And thou shalt write them upon the door posts of thy house, and upon thy gates." [10]

4. Routine prayers

Even mechanical prayer may have its value. For it is the intention and not the words that matters. Thus Rabbi Levi Yitzhok of Berditschev once noticed busy merchants rushing through the morning liturgy. He "mamamama, bababababa." They were naturally amazed. Whereupon he called them over but instead of telling them anything he just mumbled told them: "You don't understand what I said to you. But that is the way you just spoke to the Master of the Universe." One of them replied, "I once heard a baby in the crib make sounds which no one understood; but the parents knew what the child wanted. Even so does the Father in Heaven know what his children want." Rabbi Levi Yitzhok was overjoyed at this reply. "Right, absolutely right," he said, "the Father in Heaven knows what His children want." [11]

5. The Shekinah in prayer

The following Hassidic dicta illustrate the Jewish aspects of prayer. Note that prayer is assumed to be not petition but worship. Its purpose is to change not things but man: "Prayer is the bridge that carries man to God, but he must not, while praying, think of a reward. . . . The fate of the Jewish nation, and with it the fate of the whole world, depends on prayer. . . . The true worshipper is he who discovers the *Shekinah* in all his supplications. He acts as the emissary of the *Shekinah* to bring thoughts into words. . . . When we call upon the Lord, we should do so from the abyss of two depths: the depths of contrition for our transgressions; and from the depths of our knowledge that God is the only source of succor. . . . We need not bow down before the Lord with our body. Let us bow with our heart and keep our head erect. . . . The prayer of the flatterer is not heard. . . . Do not ask God to change the laws of nature for you. . . . He who forgives will find his prayer heard. . . . Before prayer, give to charity. . . . If you are not at peace with the world, your prayer will not be accepted. . . . A good man should intend to achieve through his prayers three things; first, to bring back doubters to the true faith; second, to assist the philosophers to maintain the true faith; third, to transform those who abuse him into those who honor him." [12]

6. *Aspects of traditional prayers*

What is the general spirit and content of the traditional prayers? The following excerpts will illustrate.

A life of spiritual growth and self-discipline and a good environment is the burden of this prayer:

"May it be Thy will, O Lord our God and God of our fathers, to make us familiar with Thy Torah and to make us cleave to Thy commandments. O lead us not into the power of sin, of transgression or iniquity, of temptation or scorn. Let not the evil inclination have sway over us. Keep us far from a bad man and a bad companion. Make us cleave to the good inclination and to good works. Subdue our will so that it may submit itself unto Thee. And let us obtain this day and every day grace, favor and mercy in Thy eyes, and in the eyes of all who behold us, and bestow loving-kindness upon us." [13]

The following prayer stresses the privilege of study and right practices:

"Blessed is our God, who hath created us for His glory, and hath separated us from them that go astray, and hath given us the Torah of truth and planted everlasting life in our midst. May He open our hearts unto His Law, and place His love and fear within our hearts, that we may do His will and serve Him with a perfect heart, that we may not labor in vain, nor bring forth for confusion. May it be Thy will, O Lord our God and God of our fathers, that we keep Thy statutes in this world, and be worthy to live to witness and inherit happiness and blessings in the days of the Messiah." [14]

7. *The Kingdom of God*

Three times daily the Jew prays for the establishment of God's kingdom on earth when all His children will unite in His spirit:

"We therefore hope in Thee, O Lord our God, that we may speedily behold the glory of Thy might, when Thou wilt remove the abominations from the earth, and the idols will be utterly cut off, when the world will be perfected under the kingdom of the Almighty, and all the children of flesh will call upon Thy name, when Thou wilt turn unto Thyself all the wicked of the earth. . . . Let all the inhabitants of the world . . . accept the yoke of Thy kingdom, and do Thou reign over them speedily and for ever and ever. For the kingdom is Thine, and to all eternity Thou wilt reign in glory; as it is written in Thy Torah: The Lord shall reign for ever and ever. And it is said: And the Lord shall be King over all the earth; in that day shall the Lord be One, and His name One." [15]

8. Affirmation of faith

The prayer which follows, recited in the original Aramaic before the reading of the Torah, is an affirmation of the Jewish faith in God's law and justice:

"Blessed be the name of the Sovereign of the universe. Blessed be Thy crown and Thy abiding place. Let Thy favor rest with Thy people Israel for ever; show them the redemption of Thy right hand in Thy holy temple. Vouchsafe unto us the benign gift of Thy light, and in mercy accept our supplications. May it be Thy will to prolong our life in well being. Let me also be numbered among the righteous, so that Thou mayest be merciful unto me and have me in Thy keeping, with all that belong to me and to Thy people Israel. Thou art He who feedeth and sustaineth all; Thou art He who ruleth over all; Thou art He who ruleth over kings, for dominion is Thine. . . . Not in man do I put my trust, not upon any angel do I rely, but upon God of Heaven, who is the God of truth, and whose Law is truth. In Him I put my trust, and unto His holy and glorious name I utter praises. May it be Thy will to open my heart unto Thy Torah, and to fulfill the wishes of my heart and of all Thy people for good, for life, and for peace." [16]

9. For public servants

On Sabbath morning this special prayer is recited for those who help maintain the religious and philanthropic institutions in the community:

"May He who blessed our fathers, Abraham, Isaac and Jacob, bless all this holy congregation together with all other holy congregations: them, their wives, their sons and daughters and all that belong to them; those also who unite to form synagogues for prayer, and those who enter therein to pray; those who give lamps for lighting, and wine for *Kiddush* and *Habdalah,* bread for wayfarers and charity to the poor, and all such as occupy themselves in faithfulness with the needs of the community. May the Holy One, blessed be He, give them their recompense. May He remove from them all sickness, heal all their body, forgive all their iniquity, and send blessing and prosperity upon all the works of their hands, as well as upon all Israel, their brethren, and let us say, Amen." [17]

10. For a good life

The Jew prays not only for more life but for a good life, and this prayer announcing a new month, indicates the Jewish concept of "the good life."

"May it be Thy will, O Lord our God and God of our fathers, to renew unto us this coming month for good and for blessing. O grant us long life, a life of peace, of good, of sustenance, of bodily vigor, a life marked by the fear of Heaven and the dread of sin, a life free from shame and reproach, a life of prosperity and honor, a life in which the love of Torah and the fear of Heaven shall cleave to us, a life in which the desires of our heart shall be fulfilled for good. Amen." [18]

11. One World

Standing before his God on the New Year's Day the Jew prays for a new world—a united humanity ruled by justice. He prays not for vengeance on his persecutors but for the eradication of evil.

"Now, therefore, O Lord our God, impose thine awe upon all Thy works, and Thy dread upon all that Thou hast created, that all Thy works may fear Thee, that they may all form one league to do Thy will with a perfect heart. . . . Then shall the just see and be glad, and the upright shall exult, and the pious triumphantly rejoice, while iniquity shall close her mouth, and all wickedness shall be wholly consumed like smoke, when Thou makest the dominion of arrogance to pass away from the earth." [19]

12. Accepting God's will

While the following is not a standard prayer, it is considered a very fine example of Jewish prayers, and is recited by many on the Eve of Yom Kippur.

"Oh God, I stand before Thee, knowing all my deficiencies, overwhelmed by Thy greatness and majesty. But Thou hast commanded me to pray to Thee, and hast suffered me to offer homage to Thine exalted name according to the measure of my knowledge, and to lay my supplication before Thee. Thou knowest best what is for my good. If I recite my wants, it is not to remind Thee of them, but only so that I may understand better how great is my dependence upon Thee. If, then, I ask Thee for the things that make not for my well-being, it is because I am ignorant; Thy choice is better than mine, and I submit myself to Thine unalterable decrees and Thy supreme direction." [20]

Questions for Discussion

1. What effect has the daily recitation of the *Shema* had on Jewish history?
2. What are the traditional symbols associated with the doctrines expressed in the *Shema?*
3. Was there any relationship between the traditional prayers and the development of religious schools and *Bote-Midrashim* in the Jewish communities?
4. Are prayers for the privilege of study common in non-Jewish liturgies?
5. What is your conception of prayer?
6. What is the Jewish conception of the Kingdom of God as expressed in the traditional prayers?
7. What is the value of prayers in Hebrew?

CHAPTER VIII

The Synagogue

1. Its origin and scope

"A unique creation of Judaism is the Synagogue, which made Torah° the common property of the entire people. Devised in the Exile as a substitute for the Temple, it soon eclipsed it as a religious force and a rallying point for the whole people, appealing through the prayers and Scriptural lesson to the congregation as a whole. The Synagogue was limited to no one locality, as was the Temple, but raised its banner wherever Jews settled throughout the globe. It was thus able to spread the truths of Judaism to the remotest parts of the earth, and to invest the Sabbath and Festivals with deeper meaning by utilizing them for the instruction and elevation of the people. What did it matter, if the Temple fell a prey to the flames for a second time, or if the whole sacrificial cult of the priesthood with all its pomp were to cease? The soul of Judaism lived indestructibly in its House of Prayer, Assembly and Learning." [1]

2. Bet Ha-Tefilah

The Jew laid special value on public worship, over and above private devotions:

"Said the Holy One, blessed be He: He who pursues Torah and charitable acts and prays with the congregation, I consider it as if he redeemed Me and my children from among the nations." [2]

"He who has a synagogue in his community and he does not attend its services is considered a bad neighbor." [3] It is a great virtue to be counted among the first ten of the *Minyan*. So great was the importance of praying with a *Minyan* considered, that Rabbi Eliezar freed his slave in order to be able to count him to the *Minyan*.[4]

The Synagogue was the institution which preserved and developed Israel's lofty ideals. Functioning properly it must hold up ever higher and higher standards—the highest in the community. Hence the dictum: "A city the roofs of whose private houses tower above that of the synagogue will not long prosper." [5]

"One of the most effective instruments for preserving the Jewish consciousness is public worship. . . . The service of the Synagogue is something more than an expression of the needs and emotions of the individual worshippers who take part in it. It is an expression of the joys and sorrows, a proclamation of the hopes and ideals of Israel. . . . For the Synagogue is the one unfailing well-spring of Jewish feeling. There we pray together with our brethren, and in the act become participators in the common sentiment, the collective conscience, of Israel. There we pray with a mightier company still, with the whole house of Israel. We become members of a far greater congregation than that of which we form a physical part. We join our brethren in spirit all over the world in their homage to the God of our people." [6]

3. Bet Ha-Keneset

The historic synagogue is not only a *Bet Ha-Tefilah*, "a House of Prayer." It is also a *Bet Ha-keneset*, "a House of Assembly." Not only was it the gathering place for all Jewish communal discussions, but it also reflected the joys and sorrows of every Jew in the neighborhood. When a male child was born, candles were lit in the synagogue on the eighth day when the boy was admitted to the "Covenant of Abraham." A baby girl was named when the father was called up to the reading of the Torah. A wedding took place near or in the synagogue, and special prayers were offered in the synagogue for the bride and groom on the Sabbath before the wedding. To this day mourners are welcomed with words of comfort on their entry into the synagogue at the inauguration of the Sabbath during the week of mourning. The wandering poor often ate and slept in the synagogue. When necessary, the synagogue became a People's Court. A Jew who felt that he had a just grievance against another, had the right to stop the reading of the Torah at the service until he gained a public promise of redress. And justly so! What value is there, otherwise, in reading the Law if the congregation will tolerate an injustice!

4. Bet Ha-Midrash

Besides serving as a House of Prayer and a House of Assembly the historic synagogue had a third function. It was a *Bet Ha-midrash*, a "House of Study." Where necessary it housed the local Talmud Torah, the elementary religious school. In all cases the public opinion of the synagogue brought pressure upon every parent to arrange for the religious teaching of his children. The synagogue was the library and reading room of the community,—institutions which were popular in Israel many centuries before modern communities realized their public value. But what was most important, men came daily to the synagogue to study individually and in groups. Rare, indeed, was a synagogue where the sound of Talmudic discussion was not heard and where there were no groups of men studying regularly the books of the Bible and of the rabbis, the thoughts of the prophets and the sages.

Thus the synagogue was the spiritual, the social and the cultural reservoir and dynamo of the Jewish community. It was there that the Jewish will, head and heart developed. It was there that the Jew developed the ideals and the strength of character which enabled him not only to survive all persecutions but to survive on a high moral and cultural plane.

5. The fount of Israel's Spirit

The spirit and character generated by the historic synagogue is graphically pictured by the late Chaim Nachman Bialik in his famous poem, *"Im Yesh Et Nafsheko Lodaat."* In the following translation, Maurice Samuel captured much of the force of the original:

> If thou wouldst know the mystic fount from whence
> Thy wretched brethren facing slaughter, drew
> In evil days the strength and fortitude
> To meet grim death with joy, and bare the neck

To ev'ry sharpened blade and lifted ax;
Or, pyres ascending, leap into the flame
And saintlike die with *Ehad* on their lips;

If thou wouldst know the mystic fount from whence
Thy wretched brethren drew (while crushed betwixt
Bleak hellish steeps and scourging scorpions fierce)
Divine condolence, patience, fealty,
And iron strength to bear relentless toil;
With shoulders stooped to bear a loathsome life,
And endlessly to suffer and endure;

If thou wouldst know the bosom whither streamed
Thy nations' tears, its heart and soul and gall;
Whither like water flowed its gushing moans,
The moans that moved the nethermost abyss,
And plaints that even Satan terrified—
Rock splitting plaints, though vain to crush the foe's
Steeled heart, more adamant than rock and Satan.

If thou wouldst know the fortress whither bore
Thy sires to havens safe their Torah scrolls,
The sacred treasurer of their yearning souls.
If thou wouldst know the shelter where preserved,
Immaculate, thy nation's spirit was,
Whose hoary age, though safe with shameful life,
Did not disgrace its lovely youth;

If thou wouldst know the mother merciful,
The aged, loyal mother love-abounding,
Who gather'd her lost son's tears with tenderness,
And steadied lovingly his falt'ring steps;
And when fatigued and shamed he would return
'Neath her roof's umbrage, she would wipe his tears
And on her lap lull him to sweet sleep;

If thou wouldst know, O humble brother mine,
Go to the house of prayer grown old, decayed,
In the long nights of Tebeth desolate,
Or in the scorching blazing Thammuz days,
In noonday heat, at morn at eventide.

If God has left there still a remnant small,
Thine eyes shall even to this day behold
Through sombre shadows cast by darkened walls,
In isolated nooks or by the stove,
Stray lonely Jews, like shades from eras past,
Dark mournful Jews with faces lean and wan;
Yea, Jews who bear the weighty Galuth yoke,
Forgetting their toil in the Talmud pages worn,
And their poverty in the tales of bygone days;
Who rout their cares with blessed psalmody—
(Alas how mean and trivial the sight
To alien eyes!) Thy heart will tell thee then
That thy feet tread the marge of our life's fount,
That thine eyes view the treasures of our soul.

If with God's spirit thou art still imbued,
If still His solace whispers in thy heart,
And if a spark of hope for halcyon days
Illumines yet thy darkness great and deep,
Mark well and hearken, humbled brother mine:
This house is but a small spark fugitive
That escaped by miracle the mighty blaze,
Lit by thy fathers in their sacred fane.
Who knows, perchance the torrents of their tears
Ferried us safely, bringing us hither?
Perchance with their prayers they asked us of the Lord.
And in their deaths bequeathed to us life,
Eternal life that will endure for aye! [7]

6. The American Synagogue

In the transition of Jewish life from the pale of Eastern Europe to the free communities of America, the synagogue lost its functions as a communal center and a House of Study. It remained solely a House of Prayer. This intensified the growing gap between religion and life which is so characteristic of the modern age. Fortunately, however, there are signs that both religious and secular leaders are becoming aware that this situation is far from desirable. Many a synagogue is now endeavoring to reintroduce the functions of the House of Study and the House of Assembly into its congregational program. Thus the synagogues are serving as social centers for adults and young people's groups. They house such varied activities as scouting, Red Cross work and choral groups. They have Talmud Torahs and Adult Education courses. They have lectures and public discussions.

Doubtless this process of the revitalization and re-organization of the American Synagogue has not gone far enough. As Professor Mordecai M. Kaplan points out: "It is necessary to include within the scope of the synagogue the cultivation of whatever workaday interests Jews have in common, and whatever leisure interest may form the basis of friendship and cooperation. The synagogue should not be displaced by, but it should evolve into, the *Beth Am,* or Jewish neighborhood center. Each center should be placed under the joint auspices of the *Kehillah,* and of the Jews of the neighborhood where it is located. . . . The *Beth Am* must weld the Jews who live in the neighborhood into a concious communal unit. . . . The *Beth Am* should aim to utilize the existing need for Jewish association, and to direct Jewish creative ability upon Jewish interests, projects and objectives." [8]

"The following are some of these needs: Jewish elementary school facilities; boys' and girls' clubs; recreational facilities; adult study and art groups; communal activities; religious services and festival pageants and plays; informal meetings of friends and associates." [9]

While the basic reorganization of the synagogue suggested by Doctor Kaplan must necessarily await the long and difficult process of the evolution of the *Kehillah* organization, many of the activities and the general spirit suggested can and should be introduced as far as possible into the existing synagogue. While the forms and details of organization may differ, the historic continuity of the synagogue and its effective functioning demand that it serve in the three-fold capacity as a House of Prayer, a House of Assembly and a House of Study.

Questions for Discussion

1. What are the implications for the individual and for the community of the Jewish concept of "Minyan"?
2. What special value is there in public worship?
3. Do you approve of a more or less uniform Prayer Book?

4. Shall the Hebrew language be retained in the synagogue service in America?
5. Can Talmud Torahs long exist in a community where the synagogues do not use the Hebrew Prayer Book?
6. What are the three functions of the historic synagogue?
7. What are the major difficulties in the organization of synagogues according to Professor Kaplan's plan?
8. Do you approve of the present status of woman in the synagogue?

CHAPTER IX

Torah

1. The supreme need

As was pointed out in the previous chapter, the synagogue must be more than a place for worship. It must be a *Bet Ha-Midrash,* a House of Study, as well as a *Bet Ha-Tefilah,* a House of Prayer. For Judaism realizes that, without profound study, piety may degenerate into mere superstition and may do more harm than good. Hence, the rabbis declared, "The boorish man cannot be sin-fearing, neither can the ignoramus be pious." [1] The ideal of study is therefore supreme for it gives direction and a sense of relative values to all other ideals and practices. Torah to the Jew includes both the written Bible and the unwritten tradition, theory as well as practice, concepts as well as customs and institutions—in brief, it is the sum total of Israel's culture, spiritual heritage, and religious civilization. It gives direction and content, purpose and value to life.

According to the rabbis, Torah is one of the pillars of the world: "Upon three things is the world based: upon Torah, upon divine worship, and upon acts of benevolence." [2] Were it not for Torah, the heavens and earth could not endure. [3] The Torah preceded creation. [4] The Holy One, blessed be He, made a condition with the works of Creation and said to them: "If Israel accepts the Torah you will endure; if not I will reduce you again to chaos." [5] As the fishes in the sea immediately perish when they come out of the water, so do men perish when they separate themselves from the words of Torah. [6]

Torah is not a burden; it is a source of joy and light and strength. Happily the sweet singer in ancient Israel sang: "The Torah of the Lord is perfect, restoring the soul, the testimony of the Lord is faithful; making wise the simple. The precepts of the Lord are right, rejoicing the heart; the commandment of the Lord is pure, enlightening the eyes. The fear of the Lord is clean, enduring for ever; the judgments of the Lord are truthful, righteous altogether." [7]

2. *Likened to water*

The words of the Torah are likened to water. . . . "As water extends from one end of the world to the other, so does Torah. As water descends from above, so does Torah. As water is life to the world, so is Torah life to the world. As water refreshes the spirit, so does Torah. As water purifies man, so does Torah. As water descends drop by drop and becomes a mighty stream, so with Torah—a man learns two dicta today and two tomorrow until he becomes a fountain of knowledge. As with water, which is not pleasant except to him who is thirsty, similarly the Torah is not pleasant to him who does not yearn for it. As water leaves a high level and goes to a lower level, so the Torah abandons him whose mind is haughty and cleaves to him whose mind is humble. . . . As with water, a great man is not ashamed to ask a drink of an inferior, so with Torah a great man should not be ashamed to say to an inferior, 'Teach me one chapter, or one verse, or even one letter.' As with water, if one does not know how to swim he may be drowned; so with the words of Torah, if one does not know how to swim in them and come to decisions with respect to them, he too will be overwhelmed." [8]

3. *A gradual and life-long process*

There are grades in beginning the formal study of Torah: "At five the age is reached for the study of Scripture; at ten for the study of the Mishna, and at fifteen for the Talmud." [9] But there is no age given when one may stop. For Torah demands continuous study. It is a life-long process. Throughout life one must have a regular period for study.[10] No one acquires it without an effort. "Qualify yourself for the study of the Torah, since it does not come to you as an inheritance." [11] One must humbly go after it. "Wander forth to the home of Torah, and say not that the Torah will come after you." [12]

There is no royal road to wisdom. It requires self-discipline and hard work: "This is the way that is becoming for the study of Torah: a morsel of bread with salt you must eat, and water by measure you must drink, you must sleep upon the ground and live a life of deprivation while you toil in the Torah." [13]

4. Growth of personality

The mastery of Torah is not a matter of mere knowledge. It must express itself in the growth of one's character and in the development of one's personality: "The Torah is greater than the priesthood and royalty, seeing that royalty demands thirty qualifications, the priesthood twenty-four, while Torah is acquired by forty-eight. They are: by audible study, distinct pronunciation, understanding and discernment of the heart, awe, reverence, meekness, cheerfulness; by ministering to the sages, attaching oneself to colleagues and discussion with disciples; by sedateness, knowledge of the scriptures and of the Mishna, by moderation in business, in intercourse with society, in pleasure, in sleep, in conversation, in entertainment; by long suffering, by a good heart, by faith in the wise; by resignation under chastisement, by knowing one's place, rejoicing in one's portion, putting a fence to one's words, and claiming no merit for oneself; by being beloved, loving the All-present, loving mankind, loving just courses, rectitude and reproof; by keeping oneself far from honor-seeking, not boasting of one's learning, nor delighting in pronouncing decisions; by sharing responsibilities with one's colleague, judging him favorably, and leading him to truth and peace; by being composed in one's study; by asking and answering, hearing and contributing, by learning with the object of practicing; by making one's master wiser, fixing attention upon his discourse, and reporting a thing in the name of him who said it." [14] It is not by what he knows as by what he has become that a man's progress in Torah is measured.

Wherever you are, is Torah's class-room. If two sit together and interchange no words of Torah, they are a meeting of scorners. If three have eaten at a table and have spoken there no words of Torah, it is as if they had eaten of sacrifices to the dead.[15] Let your house be a meeting place for the wise; sit amidst the dust of their feet, and drink their words with thirst.[16]

5. *The duty to teach*

To acquire Torah is but half of one's duty. We must also transmit it. We must preserve the historic continuity of our spirit and culture. Said the rabbis: "He who withholds a lesson from his pupils, robs him of the heritage of his fathers." [17] "He who teaches Torah to the child of another, is as if he gave birth to him." [18] "Look out for the children of the poor, for out of them will come forth Torah." [19]

The School of Shammai said: "Discriminate in your choice of pupils. Teach only him who is brilliant and humble and of a prominent and prosperous family." But the School of Hillel, which represents the officially accepted view in Judaism, urged democracy in education: "Teach everyone, for many a sinner in Israel was brought in contact with Torah and produced many righteous, pious and correct men." [20]

It is a sacred privilege to teach a child. It is best to study in one's youth. "The world exists on the breath of the children at study in school." [21] "He who learns as a child is like ink written on new paper. But if one learns as an old man it is like writing on an erased paper." [22]

6. *The way of the wise*

The world is a school and all men are teachers. To learn properly we must be humble and industrious:

Who is wise? He who learns from all men.[23] He who studies and does not review is like one who plants and does not harvest.[24] It is better to know more about less than to know less about more.[25] He who is bashful (to ask questions) will not learn.[26] Where there is no Torah there are no manners, where there are no manners there is no Torah . . . where there is no meal there is no Torah, where there is no Torah there is no meal.[27]

There are seven distinguishing marks of an uncultured man and seven of a wise man: The wise man does not speak before him who is greater than he in experience, and does not interrupt the speech of his colleague; he is not hasty to answer; he questions according to the subject matter, and answers to the point; he speaks upon the first thing first, and upon the last, last; regarding that which he has not understood he says, "I do not understand this," and he acknowledges the truth. The reverse of this marks the uncultured man.[28]

7. The classic Jewish curriculum

"The material which the *Talmid Hakam* (the Disciple of the Wise) was expected to assimilate embraced all branches of human learning. But just as the whole of life was dedicated to religion, so the sciences were drawn into the circle of the intellectual activities pursued by the *Talmid Hakam*. . . . The observation of nature is in a certain sense held to be a religious practice, because in ancient times the Jewish calendar was not fixed, and thorough mathematical and astronomical knowledge was needed by the *Talmid Hakam* in order that he might make calculations for the calendar. . . . Comprehensive knowledge of the animal and the plant world was indispensable for one who sought to investigate and become acquainted with the Halaka (traditional legal and ritualistic material) in its widest scope. There are entire tractates of the Mishna, the understanding of which presupposes a thorough knowledge of natural history. . . . Many *Talmide Hakamim* were physicians, and this is probably to be explained by the fact that the anatomy of the human body and of the animals formed an important subject in the scheme of their study, since a comprehension of important precepts was based upon it. . . . Highly characteristic of the culture of the *Talmid Hakam* is his attitude towards foreign languages. The Hellene looked down with scorn upon every non-Hellene, whom he simply called 'barbarian.' . . . Our old teachers, however, were spared the one-sidedness of their non-Jewish contemporaries, and these so-called dry-as-dust jurists show in their utterances a finer understanding of the peculiarities of foreign languages than did the professional aesthetes of classical literature. 'There are four languages,' remarked a rabbi of the third century, 'that one ought to use: Greek for the art of poetry, Latin for the terms of military command, Aramaic for elegies, and Hebrew for daily speech.' " [29]

8. Primary education

"Hand in hand with the development of higher education went the education of the Jewish child, which began at home before he was sent to school. This is in full agreement with the principle of one of the greatest educators of modern times, who holds that education is the concern of the family; from the family it proceeds, and to the family for the most part it returns. The characteristic feature of Jewish pedagogy has always been that the three chief ends of education were subserved as a unity at one and the same time. The earliest instruction kept in view at once the intellectual, the moral, and the religious training of the child. As soon as he was able to speak, he was taught Hebrew words and sentences, bringing into play his memory and his perceptive faculties, and the sentences were always of religious bearing. They were mainly *Berakot,* blessings, especially those that form part of the morning and evening prayers and of the grace after meals. . . . The morning devotion consisted of two biblical verses: 'Hear, O Israel, the Lord is our God, the Lord is One,' and 'Moses commanded us the Torah as the inheritance of the congregation of Jacob,' to which was added the rhymed couplet:

> To the Torah I shall ever faithful be;
> For this may God Almighty grant His help to me.

As the child rose from bed with the *Shema* upon his lips, so he went to bed proclaiming his belief in the One God. To the recital of the *Shema* before retiring was added the following verse from Psalm thirty-one:

> Into Thine hand I commend my spirit;
> Thou hast redeemed me, O Lord, Thou God of Truth [30]

It was even before the child could speak that the ideal of Torah was impressed upon him. Generations of Jewish children of Eastern Europe were lulled to sleep to the tune of the following lullaby:

> Oh, hush thee, my darling, sleep soundly my son,
> Sleep soundly and sweetly till day has begun;
> For under the bed of good children at night
> There lies, till the morning, a kid snowy white.
> We'll send it to market to buy *Sechora,* (Merchandise)
> While my little lad goes to study Torah.
> Torah, Torah is the best *Sechora,*
> My child's eyes will shine in Torah,
> *Seforim* (books) he will write for me,
> And a pious Jew he'll always be. [31]

9. *Educational standards*

"The educational standards of Russian Jewish life (before World War I) may perhaps be best illustrated by an anecdote which was told to the writer by a friend. The latter, a native of Southern Russia, in which the standards of Jewish education were somewhat lower, was traveling through Lithuania, which is on the contrary, known for its high educational level. A Jewish coachman by whom this gentleman was driven was muttering something in Hebrew. On being asked whether he was reciting the Psalms—which are generally recited by the lower (Sic!) Jewish classes in Russia—the coachman indignantly retorted: 'In your country they may be satisfied with knowing the Psalms; I am reciting the Mishna!' The Mishna is a code of law (civil, criminal, and ritual) upon which the Talmud is based. Imagine in any other country or nation a driver reciting by heart, let us say, the Justinian Code!" [32]

10. *Religion the corner-stone*

"Religion was the corner-stone of Russian Jewish life (which until 1918 included the majority of the Jewish people in the world),—religion as taught by the Bible and interpreted and emobodied in definite practices and institutions by post-biblical or rabbinical Judaism. In rabbinical Judaism, however, even more so than in biblical Judaism, religion is inseparable from two fundamental aspects. It is, on the one hand, not merely a matter of faith, forming a set of abstract beliefs, but a complete system of living which embraces the most significant as well as the least significant functions of every-day life. It is, on the other hand, a matter of knowledge and intellectual endeavor. Hence, practical piety and religious knowledge, or scholarship, formed . . . the Boaz and Jachin of old-fashioned . . . . Jewish life." [33]

11. *The aristocracy of learning*

"The ideal type of Russian Jewish life (remember: it included the majority of Jews before 1918) was the *Lamdan,* the scholar. The highest ambition of the Jew was that his sons (and if he had only daughters, his sons-in-law) should be scholars, and the greatest achievement of a man's life was his ability to provide sufficiently for them, so that, relieved from economic cares, they might devote themselves unrestrictedly to Jewish learning. As a well known scholar thoughtfully puts it, among Jews of Poland and Russia there was no learned estate, not because there were no scholars, but because the entire people was a nation of students. To be sure, this learning was one-sided. Yet it was both wide and deep, for it embraced the almost boundless domains of religious Hebrew literature, and involved the knowledge of one of the most complicated systems of law and profound theological doctrines. The knowledge of the Hebrew prayers and of the Five Books of Moses would not have been sufficient to save the Russian Jew from the most terrible opprobrium—that of being an *Am-Haaretz,* an ignoramus. The ability to understand a Talmudic text, which demands years of preparation, was the minimum requirement for one who wanted to be of any consequence in the community." [34]

12. Ideals expressed in life

But—and we cannot emphasize it too strongly—Torah is not so much a matter of knowing as of being. It is not an abstract philosophy, and its study is not mere mental gymnastics. The principles of life must be applied to the way of life. It is the combination of principle and practice that constitutes the Jewish ideal of Torah. "Not the discussion is basic but the practice." [35] "He who only studies (without intention of applying the fine principles into practice) is as if he had no God." [36] "The goal of wisdom is repentance and good deeds." [37] "He who has studied Torah but does not live up to it is to be held to greater account than he who never studied." [38]

Torah, therefore, being synonymous with life itself was, like life properly lived, not a burden but a privilege and a joy. The Jew cherished it for himself, for his children, for his people. He daily thanked God for the privilege. "Blessed art Thou, O Lord our God, King of the universe, who hast sanctified us by Thy commandments, and commanded us to occupy ourselves with the words of the Torah. Make pleasant, therefore, we beseech Thee, O Lord, our God, the words of

Torah in our mouth and the mouth of Thy people, the house of Israel, so that we with our offspring and the offspring of Thy people, the house of Israel, may all know Thy name, and occupy ourselves with Thy Torah. Blessed art Thou, O Lord, Who teachest Torah to Thy people Israel." [89]

Questions for Discussion

1. What is the literal meaning of the word "Torah"?
2. What does the term mean in the phrase, "The reading of the Torah"?
3. What are the Hebrew terms for "Bible"?
4. What is meant by the "Written Torah" and the "Oral Law"?
5. In view of the Jewish emphasis on practice, what is meant by the dictum, "But the study of the Torah is equal to all of them"?
6. Is there any difference between the historic Jewish concept of *Talmid Ḥaḳam* and the modern concept of a scientist or specialist?
7. Compare the old Jewish cradle-songs with some of the popular nursery-rhymes we teach our small children today.
8. In what way has the parental attitude toward Jewish education changed from that of the past? Why?
9. Compare the content of Jewish education common in America with that which existed in Eastern Europe.

CHAPTER X

Mitzvoth

1. Disciplines for harmonious growth

Complementing the ideal of Torah is the ideal of *Mitzvah*. The term *Mitzvah* literally means a commandment. But to the Jew it never had the harshness that the English term connotes. The *Mitzvoth* are man's proper adjustments to the spirit of Torah. They are therefore not a burden, for the ways of Torah "are ways of sweetness, and all her paths are peace." [1]

"Six hundred and thirteen commandments were delivered unto Moses on Mount Sinai; three hundred and sixty-five of which are prohibitive laws, corresponding to the number of days of the solar year, whilst the remaining two hundred and forty-eight are affirmative injunctions, being as numerous as the limbs constituting the human body." [2] This is a sermonic way of expressing the Jewish ideal that the restraints and disciplines of life constitute an every day task, and that the positive duties of man—as an individual and as a member of society—embrace and complete his personality which he must strive to develop with all his powers into a harmonious whole. [3]

The *Mitzvoth* were given to help man live. [4] They were given to purify man. [5] It is much better therefore to perform the *Mitzvah* out of love for God than out of fear. [6] The performance of one *Mitzvah* paves the way for the next, and one transgression promotes the next. [7]

2. The spirit of the act

Since Mitzvoth are to develop character, the person's attitude toward the act and not its details is of prime importance. For example, Rabbi Israel Salanter once saw a servant girl carrying upon her shoulder two pails of water. When dinner was ready, he washed his hands sparingly.

He was asked why he did not use more water (since washing the hands before a meal is a *Mitzvah*). He replied: "One must not be generous with a *Mitzvah* when the burden rests upon another's shoulder." [8]

The Besht (Rabbi Israel Baal Shem Tov) explained the verse "And unto Thee, O Lord, belongeth mercy; for Thou renderest unto every man according to his work" (Ps. 62: 13), in this manner: "We frequently see a Jew hurrying to the synagogue on a week-day, but stopping to purchase an article which he happens to see at a low price. He can only hope to gain a small sum in this business transaction, and the delay may cause him to miss the *Borekhu* response or the *Kedushah*. Yet if one were to offer to the same Jew many times the sum for a *Kedushah* which he already said, he would not sell it. The Lord in His kindness judges every man according to the value which the man places upon the *Mitzvah* after he performed it, not according to its worth to him before it is performed." [9]

"All *Mitzvoth* are the expression of the heart, the mouth, or a physical act. But the heart must be behind the other forms, or it is all in vain. . . . There is in reality no sacrifice made in respecting the negative commandments. For just as a reasoning person will have no particular desire to do the things which the physician forbids him, so will a reasoning person consider the negative commandments as conducive to his own good and hence not a sacrifice. . . . Thus there is a direct reward in the negative commandments even as there is in the positive, for a man finds joy in the knowledge that it is for his own benefit that he is refraining from a forbidden act." [10]

3. Study basic to all duties

"Of the 613 commandments some are obligatory upon all Israelites at all times in all places. Others are only for Israelites but not for Priests or Levites. Some are for Levites only; others, for Priests only. Some are only for a king in Israel. Many apply only to Eretz Yisroel when Jews constitute a majority there. Among these some apply to men, others to women. . . . The love and fear of the Lord is an obligation upon all at all times everywhere. The laws of *Sukkah, Shofar,* etc., apply only at certain times of the year. Some *Mitzvoth* are to be observed only when the occasion arises, as, for example, paying a laborer his wage on time. One does not have to hire a laborer in order to observe the *Mitzvah*. . . . But there is one commandment which is basic to all, and that is the *Mitzvah* to study. For only when one studies, when one knows the Torah, does he know what the *Mitzvoth* are and how to observe them.[11]

In brief, we may say that a *Mitzvah* is that which makes for human growth and for the harmonious development of personality. The opposite of *Mitzvah* is *Averha*, i.e., the going off from the right path. *Het*, the Hebrew word for sin, literally means "missing," i.e., missing the mark or the highest goal in life. Therefore, a drifter, a person who has no aim in life and who strives toward no high goal, cannot be conscious of missing anything and has no sense of sin. Hence the rabbinic statement: "A boorish man (an empty-headed man) cannot be sin-fearing." [12]

4. Problem of interpretation

The Jewish way of life is founded on Torah and *Mitzvoth,* on law and commandments, on principles and practices. But like all law, Torah needs interpretation; and like all institutions for human guidance, *Mitzvoth* cannot be isolated from living conditions and environmental changes. Not that the Jew must necessarily yield to his environment. It is man's moral responsibility to evaluate his environment and to determine, where possible, what to accept or reject. But principles and practices do not exist in a vacuum. Their expression must necessarily consider and reflect the living environment. Hence changed conditions require ever new interpretations of Torah and *Mitzvoth,* of traditional doctrines and practices. How shall we approach this problem of reinterpretation and adjustment to new conditions?

5. The Written and the Oral Torah

Tradition points the way. Judaism, it tells us, is made up of two Toroth—the Written and the Oral Torah. The popular conception that the Pentateuch was the Written Torah and the Talmud the Oral Torah, is really a historic fiction. *Realistically* the rabbis treated all laws and practices which came down to them as tradition as *if they were* the

Written Torah, while the process of interpretation, re-interpretation and adjustment of the living generation itself was the Unwritten Torah. Thus the *Torah Shebiketav* (Written Torah) gave stability and historic experience to Jewish life, while the principle of *Torah Shebeal Peh* (Oral Torah) gave it flexibility and the power of adjustment.

6. Stability and adjustment

Today, as in the past, we must have two Toroth—tradition and interpretation, stability and adjustment. There are some extreme rightists who have rejected the principle of an Unwritten Torah. They deny the living generation the right to interpret. On the other hand, there are extreme leftists who pay little respect to authority of the past. Their method is revolution rather than interpretation. The first gives no vote to the present; the second gives no vote to the past.

7. Conscious evolution

For Jewish historic continuity, however, we must have both. We must study the experiences and the accumulated wisdom of the past, and we must give due consideration to the spiritual and moral needs of the present. We must treat all of Jewish tradition—the Bible, the Talmud, the Responsa and all of our traditional institutions, as a Written Torah. And we must interpret, adjust and expand it to meet the needs of our generation even as the sages of the Talmud did with the Written Torah of their generation. It is only by such an interaction of the past and the present that Jewish life may look forward to a morally sound and spiritually creative future.[13]

Questions for Discussion

1. Define *Mitzvah* in your own words.
2. Is the charge that the Jew is interested only in the letter of the Law (*Mitzvah*) but not in its spirit, justified? Give examples.
3. What is more important, the quality or the quantity of *Mitzvoth* observed?
4. Does the reduction in the quantity of the *Mitzvoth* necessarily raise the quality?

5. Is the spirit of a festival superior when it has more ceremonials or fewer ceremonials associated with it? Give examples.
6. Define "Sin" in your own words.
7. Is there any act which is intrinsically always sinful, or always right, or do the circumstances make it sinful or right?
8. What does the Jew consider the greatest sin? What is the highest · *Mitzvah?*
9. Who has the authority to interpret or modify a traditional observance?
10. What effect do changed conditions have upon the observance of certain *Mitzvoth?*

CHAPTER XI

Truth

1. The merits and characteristics of truth

Truth is one of the three pillars upon which a stable society must be based. "The world exists on three things: on truth, on justice, and on peace." [1] . . . Only a society based on truth has the impress of the divine will. "The seal of God is truth." [2] God hates a liar. [3]

Truth is a matter of the heart as well as of the lips: While Rabbi Safro was reciting his prayer a buyer offered a certain sum for an article the rabbi had to sell. As the rabbi did not answer in the midst of his prayers the customer raised the offer. At the conclusion of the prayers the rabbi told the customer to take the article at the first price, for the rabbi had mentally consented to sell it at the price first offered. One must be truthful in one's own heart. [4]

The rabbis found in the very position and shape of the letters a symbol of the enduring power of truth and the instability of falsehood:

"*Emet,* the word for truth, consists of the letters taken from the beginning, the middle, and the end of the Hebrew alphabet, while *Sheker,* the word for falsehood, consists of three consecutive letters. This indicates that one must search in many places for truth while falsehood is the easy way. The Hebrew letters which spell the word for falsehood rest on one point, while the letters for truth are square and have a firm foundation. This teaches that truth endures while falsehood cannot stand long." [5]

The Lubliner rabbi said: "I love more the wicked who knows that he is wicked, than the righteous who knows that he is righteous. The first is truthful, and the Lord loves truth. The second one falsifies, since no human being is exempt from sin; and the Lord hateth untruth." [6]

"Falsehood corrupts the blood; truth purifies it. . . . Falsehoods are many, but truth is one. In the unity of truth, there is strength; truth is divine and will surely triumph. . . . In times of tribulation falsehood must be guarded against most zealously. Tribulation weakens truth. . . . He who adds to truth decreases it. . . . The world would be rescued from all injuries were truth its sovereign. . . . Flattery leads to falsehood. . . . The liar hates meekness. . . . Where there is no truth, there is no peace. . . . In a family where the parents are untruthful, the children oppose each other. . . . Liars are usually caused by undue fear. . . . He who possesses no faith utters falsehood, and he who utters falsehood possesses no faith. . . . No slander can touch the man who is known to be truthful. . . . He who is not proud is saved from falsehood." [7]

2. *The power of the tongue*

While the expression of truth and falsehood is by no means limited to language yet speech is the common disseminator of truth and falsehood. Hence the warning: "Life and death are in the power of the tongue" (Prov. 19:21). The power of speech raises man above the level of the beasts of the field and the birds of the air. The misuse of that power may place him below the most vicious of brutes. The "Eighteen Benedictions" of the three daily services conclude, therefore, with the prayer: "Oh my God, guard my tongue from evil and my lips from speaking guile." Judaism stresses most emphatically the evils of the abuse of words in flattery, lying, obscenity, gossip and slander: "The flatterer brings down the divine wrath upon the world. . . . A society of flatterers is despicable, and will eventually be uprooted.[8] Flattery leads to vulgarity and to fear." [9]

3. *Hypocrisy*

Hypocrisy is a sinister form of flattery. It is the camouflage of vice in order to appear virtuous. It is the characteristic of the politician who sits on the fence appearing to belong to either side. It is the ingratiating smile of the perpetual "yes-man." Definitely the hypocrite is a man not to be trusted, and the rabbis strongly warned against him: "Fear neither the strictly observant group nor those who are not strict, but beware of those who act as though they were strict—the hypocrites, who act like Zimri and expect reward like Phineas." [10]

Jewish folk-lore found in the swine the symbol of the hypocrite. "Treif vi hazir," "As ritually unfit as a swine," is a common Yiddish expression. The swine has one of the signs of a kosher animal, namely, cleft hoofs, but he does not chew the cud, which is the other necessary sign of the kosher animal. When the swine is resting in the mire he hides his un-kosher snout but stretches out his cleft hoofs for the world to see his half kosher sign. In other words, the swine is not only not kosher; he is also a hypocrite who wants to appear kosher.[11]

4. Lying

Great is the sin of lying: "Lying—stealing the mind of a man by insincere words—is the worst of seven kinds of thievery." [12] One should not promise something to a child and then not give it to him, for it teaches him to lie.[13] "God's seal is truth." If thou utterest a lie, thou art guilty of forging God's seal. . . . "Man is either ruled by truth and peace, or by falsehood and strife. He must choose." [14]

"Some virtues may be dispensed with temporarily for the sake of acquiring others. But if you dispense with truth, how will you know that you are acquiring a worthy trait of character? Perhaps you are not true with yourself." [15]

When Rabbi Pinchas of Koretz noticed a new gilded kiddush-goblet (for wine to sanctify the Sabbath), he was displeased. "Since when do we use golden utensils in our house?" he asked. His wife assured him that it was not golden but only gilded. "Then," said the rabbi, "you have not only brought arrogance, but also deceit and falsehood into the house," and he refused to use the goblet for the sacred ceremony.[16]

5. Gossip

But one need not tell a lie in order to misuse one's tongue. Gossip and the spread of *true* reports calculated to do harm to a fellow-man, is a common rabbinic example of the *Lashon Hora,* the Evil Tongue.[17] For in a way, Lashon Hora *is* a lie—an indirect lie. It tends to make a single act, word or attitude of the person under discussion characteristic of his whole personality, and that is an untruth. The rabbinic injunction, "Judge not thy neighbor until you are in his position" (Abot 2:5), was interpreted to mean that we must never talk against our fellow-men, since no mortal can possibly know when he will stand in another's position. Neither can he know the full circumstances of the case. Only God can know this.[18]

We speak today of Fifth Columnists. The rabbis referred to the gossiper as possessed of a kind of third-columnist tongue. A *Lishan Telitae* —a Third Tongue. For it injures three persons: the speaker, the one spoken to, and the one spoken of.[19]

Slander is vicious gossip. . . . Let the honor of your neighbor be as dear to you as your own. Just as you do not wish your own reputation slandered, so respect your neighbor's reputation.[20] Whoever speaks slander is as though he denied the very fundamental principle (God in whose image man is created).[21] The slanderer has no share in the World to Come.[22]

Slander is the reverse of charity, for it curses him who gives as well as him who receives. . . . "He who slanders, he who receives the slander, and he who testifies falsely against his neighbor, deserve to be thrown to the dogs."[23]

6. *Obscenity, a caricature of life*

Obscenity is another misuse of the tongue. It is also a form of lying. It may claim to represent the "facts of life." But the ugly, the sordid, the unesthetic are not true representations of human life. Man does reach out for the true, the good and the beautiful. Obscenity ignores the potentialities and lofty strivings of man. At best it takes the experience of the moment as the picture of the whole. It is a caricature of life tending to degrade it. "For him who uses obscene language and for him who listens to such talk without protest, *Gehinnom* is deepened."[24] . . . Refined language is one of the signs of a sage.[25] "The wise, what he is, he says; the wicked, what he says, he is."[26]

7. *Controlling the tongue*

The fact is that man can, if he will, easily control his tongue. "The Holy One, blessed be He, said to the tongue: All the limbs of man are erect but you are horizontal; they are outside the body but you are inside. Moreover you are protected by two walls, one of bone and one , of flesh." [27] Certainly there is no excuse for the tongue to go out of its sheltered way to do evil.

It takes two to make gossip, slander or obscene talk. If it were not for the willing ear of the listener, the speaker would not talk. But God provided guards for the ear as well as for the tongue. Man has fingers which are fit stoppers for the ear. So is the bottom of the outside ear soft, which can easily be bent to close the opening. Thus man has two physical protections against listening to what is not proper.

Israel Baal Shem Tov said: "When thou speakest, bear in mind that thy power of speech comes from thy soul which is part of God. When thou hearest bear in mind that the power of hearing comes from thy soul. Thus wilt thou be able to unite thy soul with the *Shekinah,* the Divine Presence. Bear also in mind that thy profane words are composed of the same letters of the alphabet as thy sacred words. Therefore, in the former, too, there is holiness. Bring them to their Source." [28]

8. Talkers and doers

Leaders are particularly urged to use the tongue sparingly, "to talk little and do much!" "Why did the Lord choose Moses, the stammerer, to free the Jews?" a popular dictum asks, and the answer given is: "God wanted the Jews to be freed from their suffering and slavery." A silver-tongued leader would have wasted his energies on mass-meetings and speech-making. But tongue-tied Moses went directly to the point. "Let my people go!" he exclaimed, and insisted on speedy results.

Questions for Discussion

1. What is the Jewish attitude toward a "white lie"?
2. What is the difference between gossip and testimony?
3. What is prejudice? Is it compatible with truth?
4. Discuss some popular prejudices. Can you discuss some of your personal prejudices?

CHAPTER XII

Justice

1. The affirmation of God

"Justice, justice shalt thou pursue." [1] "Do not despise justice since it is one of the three pillars upon which the world exists. When you pervert justice you shake the world." [2]

Justice is the affirmation of the Divine in man. "When the judge sitteth and delivereth judgment, the Holy One, blessed be He, leaves (so to speak) the heaven of heavens and makes his *Shekinah* dwell on his side . . . but when the Lord sees that the judge is a respecter of persons, he removes his *Shekinah*. . . . Israel, indeed, was brought out of the land of Egypt, on condition that they accept the fulfillment of the commandment relating to just measures, and he who denies this commandment denies also the Exodus from Egypt (that is, God's relation to Israel in history)." [3]

Conversely, the perversion of justice is the denial of the Divine. "He who appoints a judge who is unfitted is as though he had set up an idolatrous image." [4]

It is unnecessary to state that a judge may not accept a bribe of money; but even a non-material bribe is forbidden. For instance, a rabbi was passing over a bridge when a stranger gave him his hand to support him. The rabbi asked him why he did it, and the reply came, "I have a lawsuit pending." "Then," said the rabbi, "I am now disqualified from deciding it!" [5]

2. Lex Talionis

In discussing the meaning of the *Lex Talionis* in Scripture, the rabbis rejected the literal meaning that a physical injury is to be inflicted upon the person who damages the limb of another. They maintained that monetary compensation only must be paid. "An eye for an eye," they

61

argued, "can only mean payment of money. For the law must be uniform. . . . Now suppose a man with an amputed right arm had cut off the right arm of another, or a lame man had made another lame, to do the same to him would be either impossible or would inflict a punishment with graver consequences than the injury he inflicted." [6]

In the pursuit of justice care must be taken that the means do not defeat the ends. The verse, "Justice, justice shalt thou pursue," teaches us that we may use only justifiable methods even in the pursuit of justice.

3. Balance of justice and mercy

Justice must be tempered with mercy. For example: Many persons complained against a certain *Shohet* and asked for his dismissal. One man, however, defended the *Shohet* and charged that he was a victim of rivalries. The rabbi decided to retain him and when the others complained at his taking the word of one person against many, the rabbi replied: "God Himself commanded Abraham to sacrifice Isaac, yet Abraham later listened to an angel and saved Isaac's life. Why? Because to harm a man a command from a high tribunal is required, but to save a man the word from the lowest authority is sufficient." [7]

On the other hand, sentimentality must not undermine law and justice. "Neither shalt thou favor a poor man in his cause" (Exodus 23:3). It is one of the deep and fundamental traits of Judaism that while presupposing sympathy and commiseration with the poor and the hapless, it nevertheless fears that in a law-suit justice might be outraged in favor of *the poor man* even when he is in the wrong—the judge deciding in the poor man's favor to relieve his poverty. Sympathy and compassion are emotions that have their proper place and use, but even these noble feelings must be silenced in the presence of Justice. In this Scriptural command there is a height of conception, a sublimity of moral view, which compels the reverence of all. [8]

Questions for Discussion
1. What is the Jewish attitude toward class legislation?
2. Do the ends justify the means?
3. How did the Mosaic *Lex Talionis* advance the ancient concept of justice?

CHAPTER XIII

Peace

1. Prophetic vision

One of the greatest contributions which the Hebrew prophets made to mankind is the vision and the ideal of international peace:

"And it shall come to pass in the end of days, that the mountain of the Lord's house shall be established as the top of the mountains, and shall be exalted above the hills, and all nations shall flow unto it. And many peoples shall go and say: 'Come ye, and let us go up to the mountain of the Lord, to the house of the God of Jacob; and He will teach us of His ways, and we will walk in His paths.' For out of Zion shall go forth the law, and the word of the Lord from Jerusalem. And He shall judge between the nations, and shall decide for many peoples. And they shall beat their swords into plowshares, and their spears into pruning-hooks; nation shall not lift up sword against nation, neither shall they learn war any more. But they shall sit every man under his vine and his fig-tree, and none shall make them afraid." [1]

2. Rabbinic ideal

Peace was one of the exalted ideals of the rabbis. Said they: "The name of God is Peace. . . . The three things by which the world is preserved—truth, justice, peace—are really one; if judgment is executed, truth is vindicated and peace results." [2] "One of the virtues of which man eats the fruit in this world and the capital remains in the world to come is the establishing of peace between man and his fellow." [3]

3. Humanity is one

Racial theories which lead to strife are a denial of God's will: "Mankind started from one individual (Adam) so that the various races which develop should not quarrel with one another, each claiming superior racial stock. Even now there is much strife, although all come of the one man created." [4]

Blessed is the peacemaker. "Elijah once appeared to a rabbi and pointed out two men who would have a share in the World to Come. The rabbi asked the men what they were doing. They answered: 'We are merrymakers; when we see men troubled in mind we cheer them, and when we see two men quarreling we make peace between them.'" [5]

4. No peace without justice

But "peace at all costs" is not a Jewish doctrine. The Jew will not accept peace at the expense of justice. The Bible commands us to eradicate evil from our midst (Deut. 17:7), and the rabbis conceived certain wars as *Milhamot Mitzvah,* wars which express the divine will. A community or a people can be as criminal as an individual, and law and justice must be enforced against groups as against individuals.

Naturally this attitude may be abused. Each side in a war may claim that it is fighting for justice. Yet the test is not difficult to apply. In the first place there is the test of Abraham, when he refused to accept the spoils of the vanquished (Gen. 14:22 f.). In the second place, there is the test of "Love thy neighbor as thyself" (Lev. 19:18). The nation which plans, when victorious, to accept no spoils of war, and demands no privileges for itself which it is not willing to grant to others—that nation is motivated by a righteous cause.

5. A sad necessity

While the Jew may accept some wars as morally justified, he does not consider war as an ideal in itself. At best it is but a necessary evil, as a surgical operation might be. It has to be done when necessary, but is no reason for self-glorification. It is much better if it can be avoided. The need to carry arms is therefore nothing to boast about, nothing to glory in. The rabbis, therefore, forbid the carrying of a sword on the Sabbath day in peace time. For a sword is considered, not an ornament but a burden, a sign that law and justice are challenged.

6. Winning the peace

Peace, to the Jew, is more than the absence of war. It is a positive concept. "Seek peace and pursue it." One must organize for peace and mobilize the factors which promote it, even as one does in case of war. The maintenance of peace cannot be left to chance any more than the waging of war. Truth and justice which are the foundations for peace require eternal vigilance. When we permit little injustices and falsehoods to accumulate we undermine peace and pave the way for war.

"The opposite of peace—strife—is akin to the aperture of a leakage; as the aperture widens so the stream of water increases. Strife is like the plank of a bridge; the longer it exists the firmer it becomes." [6]

7. Duties in war-time

Truth is essential for peace. But you may ask: "How can one enjoy peace if he must tell the truth which people may resent?" The answer is: Get the *full* truth, and with the full truth peace can be established. It is the spread of half truths which lead to injustice and strife. Peace requires "open covenants openly arrived at."

What are the duties of a Jewish citizen when his country is at war? He must share with his fellow citizens of other faiths in the tasks of defending his country both on the battle fronts and on the home front. At the same time he must seek to remove the basic causes of war and to promote those forces which make for a just and lasting peace. The following excerpts from a statement by the Rabbinical Assembly of America issued in the early months of the war, indicate the Jewish way of seeking peace in the midst of war:

8. Seek peace

"In this tragic hour in the history of mankind, our most fervent prayer is for the speedy restoration of peace. The peace for which we pray is not a mere cessation of warfare. It means all that is implied by the Hebrew word *Shalom*, a healthy, harmonious, and cooperative social order. Our quest for peace is our effort to realize the traditional ideal of the brotherhood of man.

9. Eradicate causes of war

"This ideal cannot be attained without the defeat of those powers that glory in warfare and openly avow their right to conquer and dominate other peoples. . . . We, therefore, believe firmly that the victory of the United Nations in the present conflict is indispensable to the cause of peace.

"But, though victory is indispensable, a military victory is not, by itself, adequate to secure peace. If we are to achieve peace, we must keep our victory clean of vindictiveness and national self-righteousness. . . . The present hour calls for humility and repentance, for an earnest inquiry into the evils that generate war. . . .

10. Abused nationalism

"Primarily responsible for the present war is the abuse of nationalism. . . . The right of each nation, great or small, to exist, is sacred. . . . But a nation, like an individual, has no right to exist for itself alone. It must reckon with other nations and accord their rights equal recognition with its own. No nation is justified in exercising exclusive power in matters that affect other nations as well. That conception of nationhood which implies absolute national sovereignty is incongruous with the belief in the sovereignty of God. . . .

11. Natural resources monoply

"Any nation offends the sovereignty of God when it denies to others, except on oppressive terms, access to the natural resources of which they stand in need. 'The earth is the Lord's and the fullness thereof', and no nation is justified in assuming that it has an absolute title to the resources of the land which it did not create.

12. Racial myths

"In order to rationalize the abuse of the weak by the strong, where racial differences exist between them, there have been invented myths of the superiority of certain races over others. . . . Our experience with anti-Semitism, as well as our religious tradition, *which stresses the com-*

mon origin and kinship of all men, should make us eager to repudiate all myths of racial superiority and to expose their falsehood. Even as we denounce the application of the racial myth against us, we denounce the application of the racial myth as an excuse for the exploitation of the colored race by the white. . . . Equally to be condemned is the use of the myth of racial superiority to justify the colonial rule by the Western powers over the Black, Brown, and Yellow populations of Africa and Asia, the myth that these constitute 'the White man's burden.' . . .

13. Cultural dictatorship

"Closely akin to the abuse of nationalism through the assumption of racial superiority is its abuse through the assumption of cultural superiority. We are guilty of that abuse whenever we seek to impose our traditional culture on others or to suppress theirs. . . . Every nation, to be sure, in the common interest of its entire population, is justified in requiring that all citizens participate in that culture which is an outgrowth of the national life and is vital to its preservation. . . . But no nation is justified to deny to any group within it the right to those additional cultural interests which that group may inherit from its past and which are compatible with loyalty to the nation as a whole and with due respect to the rights of other groups.

14. One world

"The foregoing principles, on which depends the peace of the world, cannot be implemented unless the essential unity of all mankind is given organized political expression. . . . It is clear that some form of international authority must be established. To avoid the weaknesses inherent in the old League of Nations, the agency for exercising that authority must take the form not of a mere league but of a federal union, a body to whom the constituent nations delegate an adequate portion of their sovereignty." [7]

Questions for Discussion

1. Is it true that we can never have world peace because it is against human nature?

2. Would a war to defend "national honor" be justified by Judaism?

3. What should be the Jewish attitude toward the conscientious objector?

4. Is the term "ex-service men" as applied only to those who served in war, expressive of the Jewish evaluation of war?

CHAPTER XIV

Charity and Social Service

1. A juster distribution

The Hebrew word, *Zedakah,* which is commonly translated by "charity," literally means "righteousness." The Jewish conception of charity is an act which helps to right an unjust situation. God is the Father of all; all are His children; all things belong to Him. When one can share that which is needed by and is helpful to the other, it is a simple matter of righteousness that it be shared. Hence the rabbinic injunction regarding charity: "Give unto Him of what is His, seeing that you and what you have are His," [1] and also, "Even a beggar who is maintained by charity must himself practice charity." [2]

Charity blesses him that gives even more than him who receives.[3] To the argument of the Roman Governor in Palestine that to give charity meant to interfere with God's will to keep the needy poor, Rabbi Akiba replied that God, the Father, is pleased to see that the children whom He disciplines have friends who are anxious to mitigate the rigors of the discipline.[4]

"The world is a wheel," a rabbi once explained, "one is rich today and may be poor tomorrow. Give to those who are in need today, you may be in need tomorrow." [5] . . . Since it is an expression of the Fatherhood of God and the Brotherhood of Man, *"Zedakah"* is equal to all the other precepts put together." [6] . . . "When a beggar stands at your door, the Holy One, blessed be He, stands at his right hand." [7]

It is good to tell the poor to become self dependent, provided you offer him a helping hand. "When the rich man tells the poor man: 'Why don't you go to work. Look how well you are built, how strong you are, what fine muscles you have,' God retorts: 'It is not enough that you don't give him anything; you even begrudge him what I gave him!'"[8]

2. Self-respect of the poor

One must be considerate of the feelings of the poor, and support him without publicity.[9] One should try to preserve for the needy a fair standard of living. The great Hillel even provided his poor visitor with a horse to ride on. One day Hillel himself acted as guide and servant to his poor visitor.[10] If a man is too bashful to receive charity, he should be advanced the money as an indefinite loan, to save his feelings.[11]

3. Degrees of charity

Maimonides outlines eight degrees of charity: the highest form is to strengthen the hands of the poor by giving him a gift or a loan, or to join him in partnership, or to find him work, that he may not become a public charge. In brief, to help him be independent. It is with reference to this degree of charity that Scripture says, "Thou shalt uphold him" (Lev. 25:35).

The next degree in charity is to give in such a way that the giver should not know the individual to whom he gives; nor should the receiver know from whom he receives. The Community Fund is substantially on this level.

A somewhat lower form is a situation where the giver knows to whom he gives but the receiver knows not from whom he receives. Many of our sages acted thus when they secretly threw money into the doors of the poor.

A still lower form is an arrangement whereby the poor knows from whom he takes, but the giver knows not to whom he gives.

A still lower form is°where one gives directly, but before being asked by the poor man.

Next, is to give directly after being asked, but giving a sufficient sum.

Next to this is giving not enough but cheerfully.

The lowest form of charity is to give grudgingly.[12]

4. *The ways of the charitable*

"Everyone is obliged to give charity. Even a poor man who is himself maintained by charity should give a portion of what he receives. . . . The *gabbai* (treasurer) who humiliates a man by insisting that a man give more than he can afford, will be called to account. . . . Everything done or given in the name of heaven is to be of the finest. If a man build a synagogue let it be more beautiful than his house; if he feed a hungry one, let him give him of the best at his table; if he clothe the naked, let him give him his fine garments. . . . One should give as much charity as is needed, if he can but afford it. To give a fifth of one's property is the ideal norm. . . . In all cases one should give cheerfully, with a good heart; the giver should show sympathy for the poor, and should comfort and encourage him. . . . Even if one has nothing to give the poor applicant, he should not raise his voice to him, but should speak gently to him and explain to him that he would like to give but cannot." [13]

5. *Investigation*

"If a man and a woman ask for food or clothing, the needs of the woman are to be met first. . . . Food should be given without an investigation to all who claim they are hungry. A request for clothing may be investigated." [14]

6. *Gemiluth Hesed*

The Hebrew language has a term, *Gemiluth Hesed,* which is loftier and more inclusive than *Zedakah* (charity). *Gemiluth Hesed* can best be translated by kindliness, considerateness and helpfulness. The rabbis pointed out the distinction between *Zedakah* and *Gemiluth Hesed* as follows: "*Zedakah* implies financial help but *Gemiluth Hesed* may be either financial or personal; *Zedakah* can only be given to the poor while a *Gemiluth Hesed* may be done either for the poor or the rich; *Zedakah* is only towards the living, and a *Gemiluth Hesed* may be towards either the living or the dead." [15]

Together with Torah and Worship, *Gemiluth Hesed* makes up the three pillars upon which the world rests.[16]

7. *Blesses him that gives*

The moral force and the manifold virtues of *Zedakah* were constantly stressed by Hasidic leaders: "Through charity you subdue the body to the soul, and folly to reason. Thus you will go forth from darkness to light, from death to life; from animality to humanity. When you give aid to scholars you gain a share in their sacred learning. . . . Charity is a cure for every heartache. . . . While it is commendable to aid students of the Torah more than commoners, the latter too must be aided. . . . Arbitration is justice blended with charity. . . . He who gives a coin to the poor receives six blessings; he who shows sympathy with the poor receives eleven blessings. . . . When people do not give to charity the government takes away their money through new forms of taxation. . . . He who gives charity with a smile is truly a whole-hearted man." [17]

A rabbi was asked why we do not say a blessing when giving charity as we do when performing any other *Mitzvah*. The rabbi replied: "Were a blessing required before giving charity, one could give an excuse for not giving at a time that he is not clean enough to pronounce the prayer. Hence he is freed from reciting the *Berakhah* (blessing) so that he should aid the indigent without delay." [18]

8. *Hesed Shel Emet*

Even unto the dead one can extend loving-kindness. "And thou shalt do unto me loving-kindness and truth . . . and shalt bury me" (Gen. 47:29–30). The rabbis thereon commented that a kindness toward the dead is a true kindness indeed. Hence in every Jewish community there is a Burial Society, known as *Hesed Shel Emet* (the loving-kindness of truth, i.e., the kindness which is truly unselfish). It is the object of the *Hesed Shel Emet* society to provide for the proper and dignified burial of the poor.

9. *An ideal example*

The following story pictures an act of *Zedaḳah* and *Gemiluth Hesed* as idealized by the Jew. It is entitled, "If Not Higher," and is a translation from the Yiddish by Judah Leib Peretz:

During *S'lichot* days, shortly before Rosh Hashana, when Jews the world over pray for the forgiveness of sins and for a happy New Year, the Rebbe of Nemirov was wont to disappear.

Where could the Rebbe be?

Where, indeed, if not in heaven? Busy days these for the Rebbe, the days before New Year. Are there not Jews enough who want to be good if it were not for the evil spirit, who watches them with his thousand eyes, tempts them at every opportunity, and then reports against them? And who is to come to the rescue if not the Rebbe himself?

Everybody understood that.

But once there came into Nemirov a Lithuanian Jew. He thought otherwise. He laughed at the whole story. You know these Litwaks, opponents of the Hassidim, cold-blooded and exact. It's little enough they care about anything that's written in black and white, proof positive, and no mistake about it. How can you argue with a man like that?

"Well, where do you say the Rebbe goes during these days," we ask him.

"No business of mine," says he, shrugging his shoulders. And he actually made up his mind to find out for himself,—that's what a Litwak can do!

And that very evening, soon after prayers, this fellow stole into the Rebbe's bedroom, hid himself under the bed, and—waited. He was determined to wait all night just to find out what became of the Rebbe in the early mornings of those *S'lichot* days.

In the early dawn he heard the beadle going the rounds, waking good Jews to *S'lichot* prayers.

But the Rebbe had been awake for something like an hour already and lay there moaning to himself.

Then the Litwak heard how the beds in the house began to creak, as the household awoke from sleep. He heard the murmuring of words, the splash of water, the opening and closing of doors. Then, when the household had departed, the house was silent and dark once more, except where a moonbeam broke through a crack in the shutters.

He confessed afterwards, the Litwak did, that when he found himself alone in the house with the Rebbe, he was afraid. He trembled, but he waited.

At last the Rebbe, God bless him, began to get up. The Rebbe went to the closet and took out a bundle containing peasant clothes, a smock, a huge pair of boots, a big fur cap with a leather strap studded with brass buttons.

The Rebbe put these on. From one of the pockets of the smock there stuck out the end of a thick rope.

The Rebbe left the room. The Litwak followed.

Going through the kitchen, the Rebbe picked up a hatchet, hid it under his smock and went out. The Litwak trembled—and followed.

They went through the dark streets. Here and there you could hear the cry of Jews at prayer. The Rebbe stuck to the shadows, flitted from house to house,—the Litwak after him,—until they came to the end of the town.

There's a little forest. The Rebbe plunged into the forest. He stopped near a tree, and the Litwak nearly dropped with amazement when he saw the Rebbe take out his hatchet and begin to chop at the tree.

The Rebbe felled the tree, cut it up into logs and then into chips. He gathered the chips into a bundle, tied it with the rope, threw the bundle over his shoulder, and began to walk back to the town.

He stopped at a broken-down hut, in one of the poorest alleys, and knocked at the window.

A frightened voice asked from within: "Who's there?"

"*Yo,*" answered the Rebbe, in the accent of a peasant.

"*KTO YO,* Who's there?" the same frightened voice asked in Russian.

"It's I, Vassil," answered the Rebbe in the same language.

"I don't know you. What do you want?"

"Wood," answered this Vassil, "I've got wood to sell, very cheap." He waited. No answer, and made his way into the house.

The Litwak stole after him, and by the grey light of the dawn saw a poor, . . . and sick old woman lying in bed, wrapped in rags, and in her sick voice said bitterly:

"Buy? How can I buy? What money have I, a poor sick widow?"

"I'll give it to you on credit," said this Vassil.

"And where shall I ever get the money to pay you?" the sick woman moaned.

"Foolish woman," the Rebbe rebukes her, "see, you are a sick woman and a widow, and I am willing to trust you. And you have a great and mighty God in heaven, and will not trust Him."

"And who will light the fire for me?" she asked, "I am sick and have not the strength to rise, and my son is away to look for work."

"I'll do it for you," said the Rebbe.

And the Rebbe began to light the fire. As he arranged the wood, he recited, in a low voice, the first of the *S'lichot* prayers, and when the fire was well lighted, he was repeating the second of the *S'lichot* prayers. And by the time the fire had died down, and he covered it with ashes, he completed reciting the last prayers.

The Litwak, who had seen everything, became one of the most passionate adherents of the Rebbe of Nemirov. And, later, when the followers of the Rebbe told how, every year, during the *S'lichot* period, it was the custom of the Rebbe to leave the earth and to ascend upward, as high as heaven, the Litwak would add quietly, "And maybe higher, too." [19]

Questions for Discussion

1. How do the Community Funds and Welfare Funds in American Communities express the Jewish concept of *Zedaḳah?*
2. Wherein is modern Social Service an expression of the Jewish historic ideal of *Gemiluth Hesed?*
3. Do you know of many *Gemiluth Hesed* societies among non-Jewish groups?
4. Discuss the fact that the New York *Gemiluth Hesed* Society (Hebrew Free Loan Society) lends money without interest to all, regardless of the creed or color of the applicant..
5. From the above Hassidic story by Peretz, how would you describe the Jewish concept of saintliness?

CHAPTER XV

Hospitality

1. Care of the stranger

One form of *Gemiluth Hesed* (reciprocating loving-kindness) is hospitality. To love the stranger is one of the commandments in the Bible (Lev. 19:34), and the care of the stranger was throughout the centuries considered a lofty ideal in Israel. It is considered one of the acts the fruit of which one eats in this world and the capital remains for him in the World to Come. Father Abraham is pictured as the kind host whose tent was open on all four sides to receive all wayfarers. Rebekah was chosen for her hospitality (Gen. 24). It was told of Rab Huna that when he used to sit down to a meal, he opened the doors and exclaimed: "Let whoever is in need enter and eat!" [1] The Jew to the present day begins the Passover Eve Seder service with the invocation, "Let him who is hungry come and eat."

Said the rabbis: "Let thy house be wide open, and let poor people feel at home there. . . . Receive every man with a friendly countenance." [2]

2. Haknosat Orhim

In the Old World where most Jews lived in smaller communities and few wayfarers stayed in hotels, to have an *Oreah,* a guest for the Sabbath, was an honor and a privilege desired by all congrègants. The sexton of the synagogue assigned all the poor guests to homes. In America there are few large Jewish communities which do not have a *Haknosat Orhim* institution, a place where the migrant poor may find free board and lodging for a day or two. There is also the Hebrew Sheltering and Immigrant Aid Society of America, a national Jewish organization, whose purpose it is,

"To facilitate the lawful entry of Jewish immigrants at the various ports in the United States, to provide them with temporary assistance, to prevent them from becoming public charges, to discourage their settling in congested cities, to prevent ineligibles from immigrating to the United States, to foster American ideals, and to instill in them a knowledge of American history and institutions . . . and to prepare them for life in the new country." [3]

3. National Refugee Service

The traditional Jewish sense of hospitality, organized on a national scale to meet a great historic emergency, is manifest in the scope of activities of the National Refugee Service which offers "a comprehensive program of social and cultural adjustment of refugees from European countries which enforce anti-racial legislation. . . . Through its New York office, it provides cash assistance to refugees, vocational retraining and employment services, and migration information and advice. Special division offers opportunities for social and cultural integration into American life. Special services are available to refugee physicians, rabbis, musicians, farmers and scholars." [4] It cooperates with and coordinates the work of local committees established for the purpose in many communities.

Questions for Discussion

1. What does your community do in the field of *Haknosat Orhim* in an organized way locally and nationally?
2. If there is a *Haknosat Orhim* in your community, do you know its budget and scope of service?
3. Do you have a local Refugee Committee? How does it function?
4. What is being done in your community to show hospitality to the men in service?
5. If an observant Jew who eats kosher has to spend a Sabbath in your community, is there a place for him to stay where he can enjoy his Sabbath?

CHAPTER XVI

Labor

1. Work, a sacred duty

It is man's duty to work. It is through the divine power given to him
to be creative, to master the forces of nature and to improve his environment, that man rises above the beasts of the field.

Judaism lays great value on learning. It stresses equally the importance of productive work. A father has to teach his son Torah; he must
also teach him a trade or profession. Study, the rabbis insist, cannot be
wholesome when divorced from the world of action. The world cannot
exist on mere theories and abstract principles no matter how idealistic.
Said Rabban Gamaliel: "Study is a fine thing when combined with an
occupation, for the pursuit of both keeps the thoughts of sin from the
mind. Study of Torah with which no practical work is combined will
in the end come to naught and bring sin in its train." [1]

2. Joy in work

The Bible exalts work and the worker. God Himself is pictured in
the opening chapters of Genesis as a Laborer. He shapes the heavens
and earth. He plants the garden. He labors for six days and rests on the
seventh. Man, created in His image, is a *Shutaf l'maase v'reshit*, a
partner in the creative process—a process which never ends. Man was
put on the earth to work, to till the soil (Gen. 2:5). "When thou eatest
the labor of thy hands, happy shalt thou be and it shall be well with
thee," [2] sang the psalmist. And this happiness, according to the rabbis,
is not only material but also spiritual. The bread of honest labor will
make you happy in this world, "and it shall be well with thee in the
world to come." [3]

3. All honest labor is noble

The rabbis taught to "love work," [4] and, before the modern era of professional specialization, they practised what they preached. Among the sages of the Talmud we find not only doctors and scientists but sandal-makers, charcoal-burners, bakers, fishers, smiths, and so forth.

No wonder Jewish sages in all ages extolled the value and virtue of labor and decried idleness: "Idleness promotes immorality; it causes idiocy." [5] "He who neglects to teach his son a trade, rears him to become a robber." [6] "A single coin earned by one's own manual labor as a weaver, tailor or carpenter, is worth more than the whole revenue of the Prince of Captivity, derived as it is from the gifts of others." [7] "Greater is he who enjoys the fruit of his labor than the (idle) fearer of heaven." [8]

"Great is work for it honors the worker." [9] "No labor, however humble, is dishonoring." [10] "Flay dead cattle in the market-place, and do not say, 'I am a priest, I am a great man, and it is beneath my dignity.'" [11] Said a great rabbi: "I am a child of God, and my neighbor is His child too. My work is in town, his in the fields. I rise early to my work and he rises early to his. He boasts not of his work, and I will not boast of mine. And if thou sayest that I do great things and he small things, I reply, 'Have we not learned that it matters not whether a man accomplishes much or little, if only he fix his heart upon his Father in Heaven (i.e., if only he consecrate to the full whatever energies and abilities he possesses).'" [12]

Questions for Discussion

1. How do you account for the preference for "white collar" jobs which characterizes social and economic life in our time?
2. What effect does this preference have upon the attitude of the laboring class toward the synagogue?
3. Under present conditions is there any social or cultural superiority in white collar jobs as against skilled trades?
4. Is the popular laborite designation of a white collar job as unproductive and parasitic, true?

CHAPTER XVII

Employer and Employee

1. Labor legislation

From the biblical commandment not to withhold the worker's pay at the end of the day,[1] down to the latest pronouncements of rabbinic organizations, Judaism has been insisting on a just relationship between employer and employee. The worker is to labor honestly and the employer is always to remember that the worker is his brother.

According to rabbinic law, he who engages workmen is not permitted to order them to work more than the standard number of hours. Where it is the custom to feed the workmen, he must feed them; where it is the custom to supply them with a dessert after their meal, he should do so. He must respect the prevailing standard.[2]

The employee, in his turn, is obligated to give the full contracted time in honest labor. Not to give his employer of the best he can do, is as much deceit as for a shopkeeper to sell short measure. It is told of a certain rabbi who was a builder that he declined to come down from the scaffolding to answer a legal question which was asked of him. "I cannot come because I am hired by the day," he explained. The time belonged to his employer.[3]

2. Protecting the underprivileged

Humane considerations rather than the letter of the law, is urged upon the employer. Thus, the porters engaged by Rabbah Bar Chanah broke a cask of wine belonging to him, and as a penalty he took their coats from them. They complained to Rab who ordered Rabbah to restore their coats. He asked, "Is that the law?" Rab replied, "It is, for it is written (Prov. 2:20) 'That thou mayest walk in the way of good men.'"

Rabbah gave them their coats. The workers then said, "We are poor and have worked hard all day and are hungry; we are destitute." Rab replied, "Yes, for it is written, 'And keep the paths of the righteous.' " [4] In other words, in the relationship of employer and employee there must be more than the letter of the law. There is a higher law—the law of considerateness and humaneness. Where the two parties are not equally situated one must often stretch a point in order to attain a balance expressive of the proper relationship between men, all of whom are created in the image of God.

The fine distinctions in rabbinic law indicate the extent to which they went to preserve the humane element in all these relations. If a workman, for example, contracts to work for a certain definite period of time, he can break his contract because in contracting his time he is depriving himself of his human freedom. When a skilled laborer, however, or the contractor, agrees to complete a definite piece of work without any particular regard to time, he may not break his agreement, because here he does not sell his freedom. [5]

"To the charge of the labor leader of our day that organized religion is against the workingman, Judaism can plead not guilty. It is, alas, tragic irony that to a large extent the Jewish working masses have forgotten the interest which Judaism has always displayed in their behalf. In the old Jewish life, any aggrieved worker could even stop the regular service in the synagogue, present his grievance against the employer before the entire congregation, and demand a promise of redress before the Scriptural lesson could be read." [6]

Questions for Discussion

1. What should be the Jewish attitude toward the practice of some labor unions to restrict the daily output of each worker? (For example, bricklayers to lay no more than a certain number of bricks per day.)
2. From the view-point of Judaism is the demand on the part of labor for organized bargaining, justifiable?
3. When the cost of living is rising, is an employer justified in refusing the demands of the employees for an increased wage before the expiration of the contract between the employer and his employees?
4. Under what conditions is a strike not justified?

CHAPTER XVIII

Business Standards

1. No special business instinct

Contrary to popular opinion, Jews are not businessmen by instinct and they do not take to commerce as a "duck takes to water." Israel in Palestine was an agricultural people. In fact, in the course of over a thousand years which covered the first and the second Jewish commonwealth, the Jews failed to build up a merchant marine or to develop a comprehensive monetary system, two essentials for a people situated on the coast and engaged in commerce. The prophets usually looked with suspicion on the growth of commercial traffic, and throughout the centuries of the Diaspora the Jew looked back with nostalgia to his agricultural state. To the present day he observes the ancient agricultural festivals—the Fruit and Harvest Festivals and the New Year for Trees. But there was business even in earliest times, and later restrictive laws forced the Jew more and more into the world of commerce. At all times the Bible and the Codes held up for him certain business ideals and ethical standards.

2. Honesty a prime responsibility

Commenting on the biblical verse, "If thou wilt do that which is right in His eyes" (Exod. 15:26), the rabbis said that it teaches us that he who acts honestly in business is popular with his fellow-men and he is judged as though he had fulfilled the whole of the Torah.[1] What is the first question a man is asked when he appears before the Great Tribunal to account for his life on earth? This: "Have you been honest in your transactions?"[2]

3. Accepted standards

The Bible enjoins strict honesty in commerce. "As you use measures of length, weight, or capacity, you must have accurate balances, accurate weights, and an honest measure for bushels and gallons."[3] The shop keeper must wipe his measure twice a week, his weights once a week, and his scales after every weighing. . . .[4] In dividing a field among partners one should not measure for one in summer and for another in winter (because of drying up and contraction of the measuring line); one may not keep his weights in salt, or make the liquid produce a foam.[5]

It is generally assumed that one buys and sells according to the terms accepted locally. Hence any deviation, unless clearly and specifically stipulated and explained, is deceptive and dishonest: In a locality where it is the custom to give a heaped measure, and the seller says, "I will give exact measure, and reduce the price," or in a place where the practice is to give an exact measure and he says, "I will give a heaped measure and increase the price," he may not do so. It is a violation of the command to have a perfect and just measure (Deut. 25: 15). Neither may one give exact weight where the practice is to give overweight, and vice versa, in the same manner.[6]

4. Cornering the market

Cornering or unsettling the market is considered an unpardonable moral offense: "Of them who store up the produce (to raise prices), who practice usury, and who unsettle the market, Scripture declares, 'The Lord hath sworn by the excellency of Jacob: Surely I will never forget any of their deeds (Amos 8:7).'"[7]

5. A word is a bond

The Rabbis taught: The Holy One, blessed be He, hates a person who says one thing with his mouth and another in his heart.[8] With the righteous their yea is yea and their nay is nay.[9] There are seven kinds of thieves, and chief of all is he who deceives his neighbor.[10]

6. *Honesty regardless of policy*

To an American generation brought up on the legend of George
Washington and the cherry-tree, the following rabbinic legend will be
particularly interesting: Rabbi Simeon b. Shetach bought a donkey from
an Arab. The disciples found a gem suspended round its neck and said
to the rabbi, "The blessing of the Lord maketh rich." But the rabbi ordered them to return the gem to the Arab. "I bought the donkey and
not the gem," he told them. The Arab exclaimed, "Blessed be the God
of Simeon b. Shetach." [11]

Questions for Discussion

1. Is it true that Jews do not take to crafts and trades?
2. Are you familiar with Jewish working men in your community? Are you
   familiar with the scope of Jewish labor organizations in your community?
3. Is there any moral superiority to the system of "one price" selling as
   against the system of individual bargaining?
4. Is it proper to spread stock market rumors?
5. In view of the traditional prohibition of usury, is banking permissible?
6. What is your moral judgment on "Honesty is the best policy"?

CHAPTER XIX

The Good Life

1. Need for independence

Judaism considers the good life that life which enjoys economic independence and possesses a sense of social interdependence.

The dignity of human personality demands that a man stand on his own feet. As the rabbis pointed out: "He who depends on the table of others, his world is dark; his life is no life.[1]. . . When a man becomes dependent on others his face changes color.[2] A man prefers one measure of his own rather than nine measures given to him by others." [3]

The ancient commentators saw in the story of the behavior of the dove which Noah sent out after the flood (Gen. 8: 11) a parable on the desirability of independence. The dove returned with an olive-leaf in its mouth. It was a symbolic plea on the part of the bird, praying: "O Lord, let my food be as bitter as this leaf but given by Thee, rather than the sweetest of morsels handed out by a fellow-mortal." [4]

2. Debt to society

While a man should endeavor to be independent and self-reliant, he must at the same time realize that no matter how creative and productive he may be, he does not stand alone. Much of what he is and what he has he owes to others—to society and to the contributions of former generations, not to mention the gifts of those abilities, powers and special aptitudes with which God has endowed him. A man must realize his own worth—what he owes to himself. But he should also realize what he owes to others. Hence the dictum of Hillel: "If I am not for myself, who will be for me? And being only for myself, what am I?", and he added: "Separate not thyself from the community." [5]

85

3. Social heritage

The self-made man who worships his maker, is not the Jewish ideal. For no man is truly self-made. Most of what one enjoys is the product of others, the accumulated wealth of generations. "Let each person say," the rabbis advised, "how much labor Adam (primitive man) must have expended before he obtained bread to eat! He plowed, sowed, reaped, piled up the sheaves, threshed, winnowed, picked the grain, sifted the flour, kneaded and baked before he had bread to eat; but I get up in the morning and find the bread all ready for me. And how much labor must he have expended before he had a garment to wear: shearing, washing the wool, combing it, spinning, weaving, preparing it; but I find it ready for me." [6] It is because of the cooperative effort that we enjoy our high standard of living.

4. Interdependence

We are all in the same boat, and no one may act in a way which endangers the safety and welfare of the others. We are like a company of men on a ship. Suppose one of them takes a drill and begins to drill a hole under his seat. "It is under my seat," he tells the other passengers, "it is none of your business." But he must understand that the water which would enter in his place would drown them all.[7] The present world catastrophe is a tragic illustration of the truth of this parable.

5. The socialized individual

Thus while it is man's right and responsibility to stand on his own feet, he must not forget his responsibilities to society. What, then, is the good life? It is the life of the socialized individual—the person who retains his individuality but develops and extends·it to embrace humanity. "What is the proper way which a person should choose for himself? That which he himself feels to be honorable and that which brings him honor from mankind." [8]

Questions for Discussion

1. Which form of *Zedakah* is most expressive of the Good Life?
2. How does the historic term, *Gemiluth Hesed*, express one of the basic concepts of the Good Life?
3. Can the life of a hermit be considered a noble expression of the Good Life?
4. How many of the things which you daily enjoy would you have if you had to make them yourself?
5. How many of the things which you enjoy are the contributions of men of different races and nationalities?

CHAPTER XX

The Good Society

1. Free individuals and group cooperation

The historic Jewish concept of the good life as the life of socialized individualism, is evidenced in the following social ideals expressed in the official pronouncements issued in recent years by two major rabbinic organizations—The Central Conference of American Rabbis and the Rabbinical Assembly of America. In a way these pronouncements give the Jewish answer to the question, What is a good society? The good society is one in which its individuals endeavor to live a good life as outlined in the previous chapter, and which, in turn, affords all individuals the freedom and opportunity to live that life. In addition, just as in the good life the individual must recognize his interdependence with and moral responsibilities to the other individuals, so in the good society races and nations, groups and classes must recognize their interdependence with and moral responsibilities to the other races and nations, groups and classes. Also, just as it is fundamental in the good life to respect individual differences, so it is fundamental in the good society to respect the historic differences of races and nationalities, creeds and cultures:

"In all of Jewish ethical tradition, it is assumed as axiomatic that men must live for each other, that mutual aid and human cooperation are indispensable both for peace in society and for moral excellence in the individual. Judaism has always asserted the brotherhood of man. If this concept has any meaning for life at all, it insists that man must live cooperatively for the common good." [1]

2. Class cooperation

"Contribution to the common good and not the selfish service of a class is the touchstone of all moral endeavor. A moral order in industry must achieve the betterment of society as a whole above all else. Those who labor, those who lead labor, as well as those who employ labor or invest capital in industry must alike recognize this principle in the exercise of any and all functions, rights and privileges." [2]

3. Palliative efforts not enough

"It is the tragic record of humankind that many of those who find comfort in the existing order often fail to apply themselves seriously to the consideration of the ills that plague society. It is part of the great social message of the prophets of our faith that salvation can be achieved only through the salvation of society as a whole. Instead of questioning God's goodness because of the evils in individual and communal life, we should address our God-given intelligence to the extermination of those circumstances which allow slums, vice, feeble-mindedness, poverty, degeneracy and the like to continue, with only palliative efforts for their improvement." [3]

4. Sacredness of personality

A good society respects the sacredness of personality: "The mechanization of our present age and the building of large industries employing hundreds and thousands of workers have led to the custom of regarding labor as a mass in which the personality of the individual is lost or is not considered. We who uphold a religious philosophy of life cannot sanction this practice which tends more and more to treat labor as only an instrument. The dignity of the individual soul before God cannot be lost sight of before men. Machinery and industry exist for man and not man for them." [4]

A good society must protect not only the lives but the dignity and self-respect of all individuals: "We record our endorsement of pensions for old age which give the aged worker and his wife dignity and rid them of the fear of ultimate pauperism and the poorhouse after a life of labor; sickness and disability insurance which protects the worker from poverty in event of accident or illness; of mother's pensions which prevent the separation of children of poor widows from their natural guardian and protect the integrity of the home; of special protection of the worker from industrial dangers and diseases; and of the rehabilitation of industrial cripples under the direction of the state." [5]

5. Social Security

"Our recognition of the necessity of immediate relief to the unemployed does not blind us to the fact that such measures are at best a palliative. We favor the establishment of unemployment insurance, the funds for which shall come from the state and industry, both of which must assume the responsibility which is theirs for those who serve society by their labor. We favor the enactment of old-age pensions so that those who have toiled may, when their period of economic usefulness is ended, live in dignity and comfort." [6]

"Since, in the interest of human liberty, we reject an economy in which all wealth is owned and controlled by the state for one in which economic competition plays a part, we must expect that, as a result of such competition, some persons will be dislodged from economic positions that they once held, often involving others in their losses. . . . Losses result in the closing of the plants or the discharge of great numbers of employees who cannot immediately find another job. Private philanthrophy is inadequate to meet this situation and a public dole is both degrading and inefficient. Obviously there is needed a device for distributing more equitably the risks of our competitive economy. Unemployment insurance and other forms of social security are social devices to achieve this end and merit support." [7] The Social Security legislation is a great step forward in this direction. It must be developed and extended to include the areas which are not covered by the present legislation and to offer more adequate security.

6. Just distribution of natural resources

In a good society wealth is recognized as a cooperative contribution, and society must assume its moral stewardship: "When Judaism teaches the divine creation of the world, it points explicitly and implicitly to the attitude that God intended the world's resources to be used in the interest of all mankind. This attitude is affirmed again and again throughout Jewish tradition. The natural resources of the world are a divine gift to mankind. Each generation inherits vast stores of wealth which all society has slowly accumulated. No single individual contributes to the sum of the world's goods more than an infinitesimal share. From all these considerations it follows that the wealth of the world should be used socially. Nor has any individual the right to own without social responsibility what all have created and what all must use. Such concentration of wealth is an abuse of the right to private property. It is the equivalent of an unjustifiable expropriation of the great masses of mankind." [8]

7. Labor's right to organize

"We believe that the denial of the right of workers to organize and form group association so that they may be treated as economic equals with their employers is tantamount to a curtailment of human freedom. For that reason we favor the unionization of all who labor. We demand legislation to protect labor in its right to bargain collectively with its employers through representatives of its own choice without any pressure or influence to be exerted by the employers on the organization of the workmen for such purposes or on the choice of their representatives." [9]

"The same rights of organization which rest with employers rests also with those whom they employ. Modern life has permitted wealth to consolidate itself through organization into corporations. Trade organizations for mutual benefit within specific industries are quite common among employers. Workers have the same inalienable right to organize according to their own plan for their common good and to bargain collectively with their employers through such honorable means as they may choose." [10]

8. Arbitration

Differences are settled in a good society by discussion and arbitration and not by open conflict or dictatorship: "In conformity with the principle of the welfare of society as fundamental, we record our adherence to the principle of the arbitration of industrial disputes rather than resort to open conflict. In any break in industrial relations the moral responsibility for the evils that ensue rests with that group which refuses to enter into the orderly processes of arbitration and mediation." [11]

"Jewish labor unions in the clothing industry have been pioneers in the movement for drawing up written agreements between workers and employers that provide for orderly periodic adjustments of conflicting interests which reduce the danger of wasteful strikes and the bitterness engendered by class warfare. This is what is meant by *constitutionalism in industry* and should be encouraged as an alternative to internecine class struggle which is neither just nor economically efficient." [12]

9. Rights of all classes

"As we claim the right to freedom for the individual, so we claim it for all groups of men united in voluntary association. Especially do we claim for social minorities the right to organize and express collectively their group aspirations, whether they be minorities of race, color, religion, political outlook or culture. We protest, however, against the abuse of these liberties by groups who take advantage of them to seek power with the view ultimately to curtailing for others the very liberties they demand for themselves. We condemn all discrimination in employment whether by open or devious methods on the basis of differentiation by national origin, creed or color. We protest against the political and social disfranchisement in America of the Negro and the Oriental." [13]

10. No totalitarianism

A good society demands free individuals. Hence it is opposed to any class-dictatorship. "The practice of Judaism requires devotion to the democratic ideal. We repudiate all forms of totalitarianism and dictatorship of the right or of the left. We emphasize the constitutional guarantees of freedom contained in the American Bill of Rights." [14]

11. A cooperative economy

A good society demands a cooperative economy, international peace, and no economic, social or political discriminations against any race or creed: "We hold that only a cooperative economy, only one which has for its objective the enrichment of all rather than profit for a few—only such an economy can be moral, can elevate man and can function successfully." [15]

"We await and shall labor in behalf of that society in which all men shall be free and protected against all forms of oppression and exploitation. We look to that social order which shall be based on human cooperation rather than on competition inspired by greed, and in which the wealth of human and natural resources shall be used for the good of all men and make possible self-fulfillment to each human being. We are committed to the cause of international peace and its attainment." [16]

Questions for Discussion

1. Is the teaching of class-consciousness conducive to the development of a good society?
2. Is it true that the average person is economically class-conscious?
3. How does the right of labor to organize help the establishment of a good society?
4. Is compulsory arbitration justified?
5. May the right of any group to freedom of speech be limited, and, if so, under what conditions?
6. In a good society does any group have a right to claim for itself the right which it would deny to others?
7. What are the moral objections to totalitarianism and class-dictatorship?

CHAPTER XXI

Leaders

1. Leadership—a sacred service

The socialized individual will respond to the call of communal co-operation. But often he must not wait for the call. He must issue it. "Where there are no men, be thou the man." It may be difficult; it requires sacrifices, but he who refuses to act his part because of personal convenience, is guilty of destroying the community.[1]

True leadership may offer more heartaches than honors. Nevertheless it is a blessed privilege to be able to serve one's people and community. "When Moses appointed the elders he said to them: 'Heretofore you belonged to yourselves, but from now on you belong to the people.[2] . . . You must ever be prepared to have them curse you or cast stones upon you.' At the same time Moses complimented them on their office: 'Hail to you that are deemed worthy by God for this office.' "[3]

2. Leaders are human

One must not expect perfection in leaders. No man is a prophet in his community nor appears perfect to his generation. Comparisons are odious. Our wise men admonished: "Don't exalt the leaders of former generations in order to undermine the authority of the leaders of your day. 'Jephthah in his generation may be as valuable as Moses in his day.' "[4]

There is a tendency today in the opposite direction. Far from expecting perfection in leaders, there is fear for their expertness. The popular American suspicion against the "brain-trusters," has its counterpart in American Jewish life. It is found in the general community, and it is noted in the synagogue and even in the pulpit. It is well to understand,

however, that "the usefulness of a minister (or any other public servant) does not increase in an inverse ratio to his knowledge—as little as
bad grammar is especially conducive to morality and holiness." [5]

Leadership which takes advantage of the ignorance of the masses
and encourages it, is of very questionable honor. "It is a poor sort of
authority which derives its infallibility from the helplessness of the
majority. The authority that maintains itself by the ignorance of the
masses is not worth having." [6]

3. Pre-requisites for leadership

Faith, humility, patience and considerateness are the qualifications
for leadership. "He who cannot accept reproof cannot become a great
leader. . . . When a man is able to receive abuse smilingly he is worthy
of being a leader. . . . Good sense and calm faith in times of trouble
proclaim the truly great leader. . . . If God has given you the privilege
of being a leader, do not rebuke your people with an angry heart, but
with a soft tongue. . . . Let every man be important in your eyes,
and not inconsequential. For you cannot know who is worthy and who
is unworthy. Man often looks upon a fellow-man as despicable and
worthless, but God looks into the heart." [7]

A leader must recognize the actual and potential contribution of
everyone. We read (II Kings, 3:15): "And it came to pass when the
minstrel played, that the hand of God came upon him." The musician,
the leader of the orchestra, knows that great melodies are obtained by
giving each instrument its due place and credit. So must the communal
leader give each man his due credit. The will, the Lord's inspiration,
comes to the leader to assist him to achieve a harmonious goal. [8]

A leader should approach his task in the spirit expressed in the prayer
of the masters of the Jewish academies when they entered upon their
duties: "May it be Thy will, O Sovereign of the Universe, that no evil
arise at our hands; that we neither fall into error nor cause others to
stumble; and that our endeavors lead to an increase of amity and fellowship." [9]

A leader must have faith, but it must be a dynamic faith—a faith combined with a sense of direction. "Instead of indulging in the conven-

tional platitudes about Israel having survived so many of the ancient nations and civilizations, Jewish leadership should assume the responsibility for indicating specifically what Judaism must do today in order to survive." [10]

4. Vision and courage

· The great need of our generation is a leadership endowed with the prophetic vision and courage. We need leaders who priest-like know how to preserve our historic heritage. But in this era of change and reconstruction we need even more leaders with prophetic vision to evaluate the tradition and to point the way to new moral and social expressions of the creative, historic Jewish spirit. "Whereas the function of the priest has been to maintain the status quo of spiritual attainment, the prophet, the philosopher and the mystic have contributed, each in his own way, to the development of moral and spiritual values. . . . Whenever an upheaval in social and cultural life makes the traditional religion inoperative, it is necessary for the prophetic type of activity to assert itself in the conative expression of the spiritual life in order to bring about a readjustment in the moral and social standards. The philosopher and the mystic then follow with their activity, and consolidate in intellectual and emotional terms the result of the change that is effected in individual conduct and in social institutions." [11]

Questions for Discussion

1. Is one justified in refusing an office because he does not want to make enemies?
2. Must one be perfect in order to assume an office?
3. Under what conditions is one justified in refusing an office?
4. Is the refusal to accept an office necessarily an expression of humility?
5. Is it true that the quality of leadership deteriorates with the passing of generations?
6. What should be the qualifications for Jewish leadership?
7. Should qualified Jews refuse to accept important government offices to avoid the charge the Jews are "running the government"?
8. Is it proper for a rabbi to take an active part in any political campaign?

CHAPTER XXII

The Use and Abuse of Money

1. Poverty no virtue

Judaism stresses the ideal of help to and respect for the poor. But, unlike some religious denominations, it never held up poverty as an ideal to strive for. It was not blind to the great suffering poverty often brings. "The poor man is often like one dead." [1] While poverty may generate the great virtue of humility, it may also raise the temptation of dishonesty and a rebellious spirit. "The petty worries of poverty undermine man's own will and cause him to transgress the divine will." [2] What is more, poverty is not always humble. It may rebound as an inferiority complex assuming a very obnoxious arrogance. "Nothing is so intolerable as an arrogant pauper and a rich flatterer." [3]

2. Wealth not idolized

But neither wealth nor the wealthy is blindly idolized. "Not everyone who does big business is necessarily wiser thereby." [4] "More business, more worry." [5] The accumulation of wealth is not proof of the individual's special virtues. "Life, children and sustenance, are a matter of luck." [6] Greed for money can never be satisfied: "He who has a hundred, wants two hundred." [7] You cannot take it with you. "When a person enters the world his hands are clenched as though to say, 'Everything is mine; I will inherit it all.' When he departs from the world, his hands are open, as though to say, 'I take nothing of all these material things with me.'" [8]

Real wealth is not objective but subjective. "Who is rich? He who enjoys what he has." [9]

3. A test of character

A man's character can be judged by his reaction to money. "In three ways does a man show himself: in his cups, in his purse, in his anger." [10]

Among the Hassidic dicta on the subject we find: "Charity cools the passion for wealth. . . . Greed for money is idolatry. . . . Desire for money degrades a man from his ethical plane. . . . Only the man of folly marries for money. He will pay for his sin by suffering through his wife and children. . . . Desire for money corrupts the mind. . . ." [11]

Money may obscure our vision of humanity: A rabbi asked his disciple to look out through the window. "What do you see?" the rabbi asked. "I see people," was the answer. He then asked the disciple to look into the mirror. "What do you see now?" "I see myself." The rabbi then continued: "Do you know the difference between the window and the mirror? Both are made of glass, but the mirror is covered with silver on the other side. We must remember that whenever we permit silver to get between us and the world, we cease seeing people; we see only ourselves." [12]

Questions for Discussion

1. Is it true that the poor are morally superior to the rich?
2. What are the responsibilities of the rich?
3. Is poverty a valid excuse for wrong action?
4. Are people poor and dependent because they are too lazy to work hard?
5. If you had considerable sums to leave in your will to institutions, which would you select?
6. What are the uses and abuses of permanent endowments?

CHAPTER XXIII

The Spirit and the Letter

1. Lishmah

"Thou shalt love the Lord, thy God, with all thy heart" (Deut. 6:5). Not the letter but the spirit of an act is what counts. "God wants the heart." [1] The highest Jewish ideal is *Mitzvah Lishmah,* the performance of a commandment for its own sake, or rather for the sake of Him who commanded it. It is only the occupation with the Torah for its own sake which is life, "but if thou hast not performed the words of the Torah in this manner, they destroy thee." [2]

2. Reward and punishment

Though the rabbis never tired of urging the belief in reward and punishment, and strove to make of it a living conviction, yet they displayed a constant tendency to disregard it as a motive for action. "Be not like servants that serve their master with the view of receiving a reward," urged Antigonos of Socho. It is a sentiment running through the rabbinic literature of almost every age.[3]

Israel is praised by God, the rabbis tell us, for having accepted the Law without previous explanation as to the rewards attached to the various commandments: "I gave them affirmative commandments and they received them; I gave them negative commands and they received them, and though I did not explain the reward, they said nothing." [4]

3. Its own reward

Religion to the Jew is never a means to another end. It is an end in itself. "A Jew does not embrace it (Judaism) nor adhere to it to escape the perils of the soul beyond the tomb, much less the retributive justice of God. Religion in the higher conception of Judaism, is not a means to that or to any other end. Whole-hearted and whole-souled love of God is its essence; its duties to God and man are fully met only when done for God's sake, or for their own sake, not from any self-regarding motive." [5]

4. *"Kawwanah"*

Mitzvoth zerikoth kawwanah, the proper performance of a commandment requires *kawwanah* or intention. This rabbinic principle is an eloquent rejoinder to the biased non-Jewish scholar who would deny so-called "inwardness"—true piety and devoutness—to Judaism because of the presence therein of numerous fixed forms and minute regulations for prayer and other religious duties. "As if," as a modern rabbi points out, "minute regulations of the religious life is in itself antagonistic to spirituality, or that it necessarily had that effect among the Jews; as if the discipline of an army or the laws of a country must necessarily suppress patriotism, or the rigorous training of the sciences destroy love and enthusiasm for them." [6]

5. *Duties of the heart*

Bahya Ibn Pakuda, the great Jewish teacher of the 12th century, said: "The science of the Torah falls into two parts: The first aims at the knowledge of practical duties, and is the science of external conduct. The second deals with the duties of the heart, namely, its hidden sentiments and thoughts, and is the science of the inward life, *ha-hakmah ha-zefunah*. . . . A careful examination by the light of reason, scripture and tradition of the question whether the duties of the heart are obligatory or not, convinced me that they indeed form the foundation of the precepts, and that if there be any shortcomings in their observance, no external duties whatever can be properly fulfilled. . . . And it became perfectly clear to me that all the roots of works which a man must carry out to please God are founded in purity of heart and translucent clearness of one's innermost thought. If anything impairs the purity of the intention with which a thing is done, the works themselves become unacceptable to God, even if they be good works that are continuously and repeatedly done." [7]

6. *Motivated by love*

Maimonides in his authoritative code states: "Let not a man say, 'I will fulfill the commandments of the Torah, occupy myself with its wisdom for the purpose of obtaining all the blessings which are written therein, for the purpose of meriting the life of the world to come; and I will refrain from the transgressions against which the Torah utters a warning for the purpose of escaping the curses which are written therein, or for the purpose of not being cut off from the life of the world to come.' It is not becoming to serve God in this manner; for he who serves God thus performs the service from fear, which is not the standard of the Prophets of the Wise. Indeed, none serve the Lord in this manner except ignorant men, or women and children who are taught to serve Him from fear, until their mind is developed and they serve Him from love." [8]

7. *Emphasis on intention*

In his challenging discussion on the character of the *Halaḳah,* one of the foremost Talmudic scholars of our day brings the following striking examples:

"Grave historians, or rather theologians, do not show deep historical insight in ridiculing the great schools headed by Shammai and Hillel for discussing the question whether an egg laid on a holiday is permitted for use or not." [9] We hear a great deal of Judaism being a view of life for which religion is law. I am at present not interested in showing the fallacy of this dictum nor in inquiring why we hear so little about the second part of the equation, to wit: for the Jew law is religion. But if it be true that religion is law for the Jews, the conception underlying Jewish law must necessarily be expressive of Jewish thought. The discussion of the old schools about the egg is tantamount to the question of the extent to which the principle of intent is to be applied. *Actus non est reus nisi mens sit rea* say the Roman jurists, and similarly the rabbis:

Actions must be judged by their intent. Since, according to biblical law, food for the holy days must be prepared the day before, the progressive school of Hillel maintained that an egg laid on a holy day must not be used because, though prepared by nature, it was without the intent of man and hence cannot be considered prepared in the legal sense. As strong men exult in their agility, so tendencies that are strong and full of life will sometimes be betrayed into extravagances. It may be extravagant to prohibit an egg laid on a holy day on account of not having been intentionally prepared for food. But of what paramount importance must intention have been to the religious conscience of the Jew if it could assume such an exaggerated form as in the case before us! And could there be a better criterion of the development of a religion than the importance it attaches to intent, the outcome of thought and emotion, in opposition to merely physical action?

8. The thought behind the act

"Now let us examine another *Halakah* that might throw light on the question as to the relation of thought and emotion to acts and deeds in Jewish theology. Sin, we are told by leading theologians, consists, according to the Jewish conception, in acting wrongly, and hence forgiveness, or, to use the more technical term, atonement, is of a purely mechanical nature. Originally there were different kinds of sacrifices, the sin offerings, the guilt offerings, and so forth, by means of which the sinner could right himself with God. Later the rabbis substituted prayer, fasting and almsgiving for the sacrifices which, after the destruction of the Temple, could no longer be brought. So far for our theologians. And now let us hear what the *Halakah* has to say about it. In a large collection of laws treating of marriage with conditions attached, which is to be found in the Talmud, we read: 'If one says to a woman, I marry thee under the condition that I am an entirely righteous man, the marriage is valid, even if it is found that he was a very wicked man, because we apprehend that at the time of the contraction of marriage he repented in his heart. If one says to a woman, I marry thee under the condition that I am a completely wicked man—sin is homely but also attractive!—the marriage is valid.' [10] For even if it is found that he was very pious, we apprehend that at the time of the contract he had thoughts of idolatry. Sin as well as forgiveness is thus understood by Jewish law to be entirely independent of acts and deeds; the evil thought in the heart turns the perfectly just into the completely wicked, and vice versa, the change of heart changes the completely wicked into the perfectly just." [11]

Questions for Discussion

1. When is it right or wrong to publicize a donation?
2. Is the routine observance of a ceremonial always valueless?
3. Is it better not to contribute than to contribute with the intention of receiving honors?
4. Are legal fictions justified? Are they justified in laws involving human welfare? Are they justified in ceremonial laws?
5. What is implied by *Kawwanah* and *Lishmah*?

CHAPTER XXIV

The Family

1. Celibacy disapproved

Judaism sees the attainment of human perfection only when the divine in man has reached complete development through the unimpeded activity of all his physical, spiritual, moral, and social forces. It deprecates, therefore, the idea that any force or faculty of human life be regarded as unholy and therefore to be suppressed. It thus rejects on principle monastic renunciation and isolation, pointing to the Scriptural verse, "He who formed the earth created it not for a waste; He formed it to be inhabited." [1]

"Accordingly Judaism regards the establishment of family life through marriage as a duty obligatory upon mankind, and sees in the entrance into marital relation an act of life's supreme consecration. In contrast to the celibacy glorified by some of the church Fathers, the Tannaite Rabbi Eliezer pronounces the man who through bachelorhood shirks the duty of rearing children to be guilty of murder against the human race. Another rabbi calls him a despoiler of the divine image. Another one says that such a man renounces his privilege of true humanity, in so far as only in the married state can happiness, blessing, and peace be attained.[2] It is significant of the spirit of Judaism that, while other religions regard the celibacy of the priests and saints as signs of highest sanctity, the Jewish law expressly commands that the high priest shall not be allowed to observe the solemn rites of the Day of Atonement if unmarried.[3] He can make intercession for the household of Israel only if he himself has founded a family, in which are practiced faithfulness and modesty." [4]

2. *Home a sanctuary*

We shall never get to the heart of Judaism as a rule of life, nor begin to understand its distinctive individuality as a religious civilization, unless and until we have grasped the great Jewish ethical principle of the holiness of home. . . . Jewish history begins with the family, with the three patriarchs and the four matriarchs of the Jewish People. No less than thirty-eight of the fifty chapters of the Book of Genesis deal exclusively with family history.[5]

The family is the foundation of the social edifice. But for its stability and well-being neither society nor the state could exist. The home is the nursery of all the virtues. "If," say the rabbis, "a man sin against those of his own household, he will inevitably come to sin against his neighbor." [6] To promote domestic peace and well-being is, then, a duty incumbent upon all the members of the family alike. Parents and children, husband and wife, brothers and sisters, master and servant, are bound together by an organic tie. Their relations are not mechanical, but moral. And the obligations that bind them together are mutual.[7]

Questions for Discussion

1. What role do children play in the moral and social development of their parents?
2. Does planned parenthood undermine the morale of the family?
3. Is there danger to the morale and to the spiritual opportunities of the family in the modern tendency of outside organizations taking over more and more the care of the children? (Pre-kindergartens, settlement houses, community centers, scouting, clubs, etc.)
4. In view of changed conditions in modern Jewish life, there is the question whether it would be wise to form a kind of monastic order for women past a certain age who are not likely to be married? What would be the advantages of such an order? Would the existence of such an order undermine the historic Jewish ideal of the family?

CHAPTER XXV

Husband and Wife

1. Marriage exalted

"And the Lord God said, 'It is not good that the man should be alone, I will make a help-mate suitable for him' " (Gen. 2: 18).

Thus from the very beginning the Jewish ideal of the union of man and wife was not a compromise with the devil, as some church doctrines maintain, but rather the completion and climax of God's creative spirit. Marriage therefore is considered a divine service, and *Kiddushin,* sanctification, is the legal term for betrothal in rabbinic literature. The Almighty Himself is said to be engaged since creation in the task of arranging matrimonial matches—a task considered as difficult as the Israelites' crossing of the Red Sea.[1] To marry and rear a family is considered the first command addressed by God to man, "Increase and multiply" (Gen. 1: 28). An unmarried man is not a man (human) in the full sense; as it is said, "Male and female created He them, and blessed them and called *their* name *man*" (Gen. 5: 2).[2] The unmarried man lives without joy, without blessing, and without good.[3] A man's home is his wife.[4] Marriage is sacred and must therefore be a thoughtful, careful and deliberate act. Considering what she can do for him, man is enjoined to love his wife like his own self and to honor her even more.[5]

2. Eugenics

Disparity in age between husband and wife was discouraged by the rabbis.[6] They greatly condemned the marriage based primarily on financial considerations.[7] The cordial relationship between husband and wife is considered a mutual responsibility, and a man is said to have the wife he deserves.[8]

Since the main object of marriage was the rearing of a family, certain principles of eugenics are stressed. One should avoid the probability of children who would be freaks or extreme. Thus the rabbis urged that a tall man should not marry a tall woman lest their children be lanky. A short man should not marry a short woman lest their children be dwarfish. A fair man should not marry a fair woman lest their children be extremely fair. A dark man should not marry a dark woman lest their children be exceedingly dark.[9]

3. Environment

While Jewish teachers often pointed out that Torah and culture were not inherited, they stress the importance of a cultural environment: "A man should sell all he possesses in order to marry the daughter of a learned man, for if he were to die or be exiled, he may be confident that his children will be learned. And let him not marry the daughter of an ignoramus, for if he were to die or be exiled, his children would be ignorant. A man should sell all that he has in order to marry the daughter of a scholar or give his daughter to a scholar in marriage. That is like uniting grapes of the vine to grapes of the vine, which is good and acceptable. But let him not marry the daughter of an ignoramus, because that is like uniting grapes of the vine to berries of the bush, which is something unattractive and unacceptable." [10]

Socially a woman can adjust herself much better than a man. Hence, "Descend a step in choosing a wife." [11] A woman of higher social status may put the man in an embarrassing position and create in him an inferiority complex.

4. Domestic harmony

Normally man is the provider and woman the home-maker. Often the provider does not see the need for all the household expenses and the allowance that he does give his wife is given grudgingly. Hence the injunction: "A man should spend less than his means on food and drink for himself, up to his means on his clothes, and above his means on honoring his wife and children, because they are dependent on him, while he is dependent upon Him Who spake and the Universe came into being." [12]

The Hebrew word for man is *Ish,* spelled *Aleph, Yad, Shin.* The Hebrew word for woman is *Isha,* spelled *Aleph, Shin, Heh.* The letters which the two words for man and woman have in common are *Aleph* and *Shin,* which spell the Hebrew word *Esh,* "fire." The word *Ish* (man) has the *Yad* not found in *Isha* (woman), and the word *Isha* has the *Heh* not found in *Ish.* Join *Ish and Isha* (man and woman) and both have the *Yad* and *Heh* which spell *Ya,* "God." Take away from each what the other has to offer, and what is left is *Esh,* "fire." Hence the comment that when husband and wife are worthily united they express God's presence; when the union is unworthy it represents a consuming fire.[13]

Questions for Discussion

1. What is your reaction to the traditional Jewish emphasis on *Yichus* (family and pedigree) in marriage?
2. Has the old institution of the *Shadchan* any place in the modern Jewish community? Where *Shadchanim* are accepted, does the woman have an equal chance with the man in proposing marriage?
3. What do you think of married women working in an office or a store when there is no economic emergency for it?
4. Is divorce justifiable? Under what circumstances?
5. What is your reaction to the traditional Jewish divorce laws?

CHAPTER XXVI

Marriage

1. Spiritual implications

"There is no civilization where marriage can take place without some kind of ceremony. What is the purpose of these ceremonies if not to render the man and the woman conscious that their marriage offers them a new means of enlarging their sympathies, developing their personality, widening the scope of their ideas and feelings, and adding purpose and strength to their will? This is what is meant by saying that God manifests Himself in the home in which the purpose of marriage is fulfilled. In the words of the Sages, 'The presence of God abides in the home in which man and wife live up to the spiritual significance of their wedlock.' " [1]

2. Sanctification

The traditional Jewish marriage ceremony which takes place under a canopy, symbolizing the home, is introduced (besides the benediction over the cup of wine) by the officiating minister reciting a benediction in which is stressed both the discipline and the sanctification implicit in the marriage union: "Blessed art Thou, O Lord our God, King of the universe, who hast sanctified us by Thy commandments, and hast given us the command concerning forbidden marriages; who hast disallowed us those that are betrothed, but hast sanctified unto us such as are wedded to us by the rite of the canopy and the sacred covenant of wedlock. Blessed art thou, O Lord, who sanctifiest thy people Israel by the rite of the canopy and the sacred covenant of wedlock."

3. "According to the statutes"

The formula recited by the groom as he places his ring on the finger of the bride in the presence of two qualified witnesses, refers to the religious and social requirements and responsibilities of the union: "Behold, thou art sanctified unto me by this ring, according to the statutes of Moses and of Israel."

4. The seven benedictions

Following the reading of the *Ketubah* or marriage contract which specifies the marital obligations assumed by the husband as well as the settlement upon the woman of certain sums traditionally fixed or voluntarily assumed, all "in accordance with the ordinances of our sages of blessed memory," the rabbi recites the Seven Benedictions over a full cup of wine. As will be seen, these benedictions stress the dignity of man made in the image of a Creative God, and of woman, part of man's very self. But they include more than that. They include prayers for the restoration of Zion, the upbuilding of Israel's national home. They remind the man and woman that they are not an isolated couple but that they are part of a larger unit—the Jewish people. The happiness of the individual home must be tied up with the happiness of the national home, and the Jewish character of the individual home will be influenced by the ideal of the national home. The Seven Benedictions are:

Blessed art Thou, O Lord our God, King of the universe, who createst the fruit of the vine.

Blessed art Thou, O Lord our God, King of the universe, who hast created all things to Thy glory.

Blessed art Thou, O Lord our God, King of the universe, Creator of man.

Blessed art Thou, O Lord our God, King of the universe, who hast made man in Thine image, after Thy likeness, and hast prepared unto him, out of his very self, a perpetual fabric. Blessed art Thou, O Lord, Creator of man.

May she who was barren (Zion) be exceedingly glad, and exult when her children are gathered within her in joy. Blessed art Thou, O Lord, who makest Zion joyful through her children.

O make these loved companions greatly to rejoice, even as of old Thou didst gladden Thy creatures in the Garden of Eden. Blessed art Thou, O Lord, who makest bridegroom and bride to rejoice.

Blessed are Thou, O Lord our God, King of the universe, who hast created joy and gladness, bridegroom and bride, mirth and exultation, pleasure and delight, love, brotherhood, peace and fellowship. Soon may there be heard in the cities of Judah and in the streets of Jerusalem, the voice of joy and gladness, the voice of bridegroom and bride, the jubilant voice of bridegrooms from their canopies, and of youths from their feast of song. Blessed art Thou, O Lord, who makest the bridegroom to rejoice with the bride.[2]

5. *Inter-dependence of Judaism and the family*

In married life it is the attitude toward the institution of the family on the part of husband and wife that determines not only their relationship to each other, but their ambitions and achievements in every one of their other relationships. What family integrity has contributed to the perpetuation of Judaism, and what Judaism in turn has done to perfect the institution of the family as a socializing and spiritualizing agency in the life of the Jew, are matters that should have been given scientific study. But we are on *terra firma* when we say that as a factor for moral purity Jewish family life has been without equal. Judaism's influence upon the attitude of the greater part of mankind toward chastity has been more far-reaching, perhaps, than upon the attitude toward any other human or cosmic relationship.[3]

6. *A communal register*

It devolves entirely upon Judaism, as far as Jews are concerned, to uphold the social and spiritual conception of marriage. . . . It must be entered into without any mental reservation about its permanence. *To further these ends, marriage among Jews must be treated as an event of significance to the Jewish community as a whole. It must, therefore, be solemnized by a representative of Jewish communal life, and re-corded in a Jewish communal register.* A Jew and a Jewess, whose union is solemnized merely by an official of the city or state, should be regarded as reading themselves out of the Jewish community.[4]

Questions for Discussion

1. What ideals do the Jewish marriage ceremonies stress?
2. Do you think that the Jewish Community Council, the Federation or some other agency in your community should introduce a Communal Register for the recording of Jewish marriages and other vital statistics?
3. Has the traditional Jewish family spirit helped Israel to survive? If so, how?

CHAPTER XXVII

Parental Responsibilities

1. Attitude toward children

Among the most enlightened nations of antiquity the child had no rights, no protection, no dignity of any sort. In Greece, weak children were generally *exposed,* that is, abandoned on a lonely mountain to perish. Public opinion demanded that deformed children be drowned or otherwise put out of the way. In Roman times, a man could at will put even a grown son to death. The respect which Jews showed for infant life and their horror at any form of child murder were criticized by their neighbors as a contemptible weakness of a perverted people. The Roman historian Tacitus, in describing the population of Judaea, says: "All their customs owe their strength to their very badness. . . . The Jews do not allow any images of the Deity to stand in their Temples . . . and it is a crime among them to kill any child." [1] It is in such a society that the rabbis proclaimed the biblical view that the child was the highest of human treasures. . . . This attitude remains the attitude . . . to this day. Let us point but to one circumstance. Jewish infant mortality is everywhere lower than the non-Jewish infant mortality—often it is only one-half of that among the general population! The rabbis declared little children to be the Messiahs of mankind. . . . In the child God gives humanity a chance to make good its mistakes. The child is thus the perennial regenerative force in humanity.[2]

2. Children a sacred trust

Children are a treasured divine trust: One Sabbath afternoon while Rabbi Meir was lecturing in the synagogue his two sons died at home. Their mother laid them upon a bed and covered them with a sheet.

When the Rabbi returned to his home at the termination of the Sabbath, he asked for his boys. His wife said, "I want to ask you a question. Some time ago we were entrusted with a treasure, and now we are asked to return it. What shall we do?" The Rabbi replied, "Certainly it must be returned upon demand." She then said, "We have already returned it. As you said, what has been entrusted must be returned on demand. 'God has given and God has taken; blessed be the name of the Lord.'" She then told him of their tragedy.[3]

3. Training for life and spiritual growth

It is the father's duty to initiate his child into religious rites, to teach him Torah, to teach him a trade, and also to teach him swimming.[4] Recalling the suffering which followed Jacob's favoritism toward Joseph, the Rabbis warn a parent not to make invidious distinctions between children.[5] While the rod need not always be spared, a grown child should not be subjected to bodily punishment.[6] Parents must not terrorize children, neither should they threaten them. Either the child is to be punished there and then, or the offense is to be overlooked, and punishment should always be accompanied by some gesture of affection. "One should push them away with the left hand, and draw them near with the right." [7]

"For I know him, that he will command his children and his household after him, that they shall keep the way of the Lord, to do righteousness and justice" (Gen. 18: 19). This responsibility placed upon Abraham, the Father of the Jewish People, was assumed to be the responsibility of every subsequent father in Israel. It was a responsibility of which the Jew reminded himself the first thing in the morning and the last thing before retiring, when he recited the *Shema*, ". . . and thou shalt teach it to thy children, and shalt inscribe it upon thy door-post, and thou shalt bind it as a sign upon thy hand and for frontlets between thine eyes."

According to a fine old legend, it was this pledge to teach the children that made Israel worthy of receiving the Torah: God asked for bondsmen to guarantee that Israel would observe the Torah. Abraham, Isaac and Jacob offered themselves as bondsmen but were rejected. The prophets were not acceptable. "We will give Thee our children as surety," the Israelites at Sinai cried. That bond was accepted and the Torah given to Israel.[8]

4. Early impressions

This important training cannot begin too early. Since "the beginning of wisdom is reverence for the Lord," it is the parents' responsibility to begin to teach him to recite the *Shema* and the benedictions as soon as the child learns to talk. They are to teach him the ceremonials as soon as he is old enough.[9] In general the best time for education are the impressionable years. "If one learns as a child, what is he like? Like ink written on clean paper. If one learns as an old man, what is he like? Like ink written on blotted paper." [10]

5. Learning and piety

Learning and piety were the ideals which the traditional Jewish parents held up for the child. The first morning prayer the child learned was: *"Shema Yisroel, Adonoi Elohenu, Adonoi Ehod,* Hear O Israel, the Lord is our God, the Lord is one. The Torah which Moses commanded to us is the inheritance of the house of Israel. I will be good and pious and will do what father tells me and what mother tells me, and what all good and pious people teach me to do that is right."

6. Lullabies

But it was not so much the formal training as the environment of the home, the example of the parents and their attitude toward learning and piety which was the most precious and enduring heritage transmitted by the parents to their children. We referred in an earlier chapter (Torah) to the old lullabies. Here are examples of cradle songs expressing the ideals transmitted to their children by the East European Jewish mothers of only yesterday, the ideals absorbed by the Jews of Poland, Roumania, Russia, Lithuania, and the Ukraine—the men and women upon whose ruthless persecution and wholesale massacre the "civilized" world looked with indifference. Not money, not banking, not great commercial achievements but character and conduct, learning and piety were the ideals. To be sure the mother was interested in wholesome food for the growing child but she was equally concerned about proper food for his mind and heart: "Toire, Toire in kepele, kashe, kashe in tepele," "Torah in the head, Gruel in the pot." And again:

> Pletslech mit piter vet'n ihm shmiren
> In Heider vet'n ihm fieren.
> S'forim vet er shreiben
> Ein giter yid vet er bleiben.

> (Buttered biscuits he'll be fed
> And then to Heder he'll be led.
> New books he'll write too
> And always be a pious Jew.) [11]

Not that the mother thinks that Torah comes easy and that Jewish life is the easiest way. She knows what pain and hardships and trials it will bring the child in the future. But she is giving him that which alone makes life worthwhile. The ideal life is the life of the ideal:

> Lernt, kinder, hot nit Moire
> Yeder onheib is shwer.
> Glicklech der, vus lernt Toire,
> Tsu darf der yid noch mehr?

> Ihr vet Kinder, elter veren
> Vet ihr allein varshtein
> Vie fiel in die Oisiyos liegen trehren
> Un vie fiel gevein.

> (Study, children, do not fear
> The many hardships which appear.
> Torah learning brings much joy
> To every Jewish man or boy.

> As you age you'll realize
> What sorrows, sadness, tears and sighs
> In these symbols lie concealed.
> To wisdom is it all revealed.)

What greater joy, what finer ideal for the traditional Jewish parents than to see their child grow up to be pious and expound the Torah in public:

> A giter un a frimer yid vet mir
> Dos kind bleiben
> "Toire Tzivo Moishe Morushe"
> Tsi der Bar Mitzveh vet er zugen
> A Drushe.

> Tsi der Drushe vet er sech shtellen
> Der futer mit der miter velln unquellen.
> Gur dem Oilem vet zein Drushe gefellen
> Gur dem Oilem, gur der velt.

> (A good, observant, pious Jew
> This child of mine will be.
> "Moses left a wealth of Law"
> To all eternity.

> When confirmed, my child will rise
> And learnedly he'll preach.
> His parents' hearts will swell with pride,
> The world will like his speech.)

What more precious treasure than a good child? What higher objective in life for a parent than to rear a saint?

> Alle brillianten un alle antiken
> Kennen doch mein hartz azoi nit erkwiken,
> Vie viel du tist es, mein licht, mein shein.
> Az ich zeh dich is die gantse velt mein.
> Schluf mein kind,
> Zollst mir riehen
> Un zein gezind!
> As die liegst un shlufst in dein viegel
> Bedecken dir Malochim mit zeire fliegèl.
> Az ich vell amohl darfen auf yener velt gehen,
> Vellen die tieren fon Gan-Eden offen shtehn.
> Die, mein kind, zollst mir zein a frimmer un a giter
> Vet men zugen auf yener velt: "Lost arein dem Tsadek's miter"

(No diamonds and no precious things
Can stir my heart until it sings,
As you, my love, my treasure fine
Having you, the world is mine!
        Sleep, my child,
        Rest in your sleep,
        Grow strong.
Lying in your cradle, sleeping,
Winged angels watch are keeping;
When I leave this world behind
Eden's open doors I'll find.
You, dear child, will a good man be
And gain admission there for me.
When I reach the world, the other,
I'll be welcomed as the Saint's mother.)

What are the ideals of the modern cradle-songs which, alas, many of our "progressive" mothers have adopted in place of the lullabies of their grandmothers? Compare the above concepts with those expressed in "Eenie, Meinee, Minee, Mo," "Little Jack Horner" and "This Little Pig Goes to Market!"

7. Parents' personal example

Torah and the Jewish way of life were the ideals impressed by parents upon the impressionable minds of their children. The personal attitude and example of the parents were the greatest forces in the preservation of these ideals. *Personal example*—this is the greatest responsibility of parents today.

"Take now your child . . . to the land of Moriah" (Gen. 22:2) . . . to the Land of Teaching . . . the land of the fear and reverence of God . . . the land of sacrifices. . . . You (parents) must take your child to this Moriah! He cannot, he will not go alone! You must take the lead in the work of revival and rejuvenation. . . . This is the supreme, outstanding problem for the Jew today. Not anti-Semitism, not the attacks of those outside our ranks should give us the greatest concern. We must never forget the truth, foreseen by the prophets ages ago, that 'They that destroy thee and they that make thee waste shall go forth from thee' (Isaiah 49: 17). Our own children—they alone have the power to lay us waste." [12] If parents want their children to follow the right paths, the first thing parents must understand is that they must lead the way and set the proper example.

Questions for Discussion

1. What example in Jewish living do most parents today set for their children?
2. Can a Talmud Torah effectively teach ideals and practices which are not honored by the parents of the pupils?
3. Is the parents' attitude toward the teachers of the Hebrew school conducive to the development of respect for Jewish scholarship on the part of the child?
4. Are you familiar with the phonograph records and juvenile literature available for the early home training of the Jewish child?
5. What are the chief responsibilities of Jewish parents?

CHAPTER XXVIII

Filial Duties

1. Honoring parents

"Honor thy father and thy mother" (Ex. 20:12). The rabbis said: "Great is the duty to honor parents since the Holy One, blessed be He, attached to it still greater importance than the honoring of Himself. With what do you honor God? With that which He has given you, as when you carry out such commandments as the forgotten sheaf, the corner of the field, tithes, charity to the poor, and so forth. If you have the means of meeting these duties you do so; but if you are poor yourself you are under no obligation. With the honoring of parents, however, no such conditions exist. Even if you have to go begging from door to door you must help your parents." [1]

Honoring one's parents is counted among the activities the fruit of which one enjoys in this world and the capital remains in the World to Come. [2]

The Bible commands children both to honor and to have reverence for the parents. By reverence is meant that a child does not stand in the parent's place, occupy his seat, contradict irreverently his statement. By honor is meant that the child provides the parent with sustenance and personal service. [3]

2. Examples of filial reverence

Not the objective act but the spirit in which it is performed and its motivation determine whether the act is or is not respectful. That son, though he gave his father a chicken dinner, violated the commandment when he replied to the father's question where he obtained the chicken, by exclaiming: "Old man, eat and be quiet; dogs eat and are quiet."

But the son who put his father to grind at the mill so as to save him from the forced labor of the invader, definitely honored thereby his father.[4]

Sir Walter Raleigh did less for his queen than did Rabbi Tarphon for his mother whose sandal slipped from her foot while she was out walking on the Sabbath. Whereupon Tarphon placed his hands beneath her sole and she walked on them until she reached her room.[5]

Yet as a shining example of filial respect the rabbis held up Dama of Ascalon, a Gentile. At one time he turned down a sale of gems which offered great profit because he would not awaken his father who had the key to the strong box.[6] Another time his mother slapped his face with her slipper while he was presiding over the assembly. When in her excitement she dropped the slipper, he bent down and picked it up for her.

In referring to a departed parent, one said: *My father,* or *mother, of blessed memory.* The custom today is to say, *Olov HaSholom,* or *Olehah HaSholom,* "Peace be upon him," or "Peace be upon her." In referring to a departed teacher we say, *Zikhrono Li'vrakhah,* "May his memory be for a blessing." [7]

As a general guiding principle one must remember that "A person's will is his honor." [8] One is not respectful to one's parents when one wilfully ignores their will.

Questions for Discussion

1. If our kashrut-observing parents cannot eat in our home, are we remiss in our filial duties?
2. Is it wrong for a man to leave the synagogue which his father attends and join a synagogue where he and *his* children may find their religious needs?
3. Make a list of things wherein we are remiss in our filial duties.
4. Make a list wherein we can best express our filial respect and affection.

CHAPTER XXIX

The Jewish Home

1. A dedicated place

"How fair, O Jacob, are your tents! How fair your homes, O Israel!" [1]

It has been said that to the Englishman his home is his castle, and to the Jew his home is his sanctuary. A castle is marked by a flag proclaiming under whose service it stands. The traditional Jewish home is marked by the *Mezuzah*, proclaiming that it is dedicated to the One God whom the men and women of the house must serve with all their hearts, with all their might and with all their substance.

2. Cemented by ceremonials

The traditional Jewish home is rooted in religion, and its spirit of holiness springs from the association of certain times and seasons with ceremonial customs regarded as sacred. "It is impossible to describe to those who have not experienced it, the feeling of holy joy which is diffused throughout the humblest Hebrew home by the solemn repetition of acts which in themselves may be regarded as mere customs without vital connection with the souls of men. Man is made of history. The Jew recognizes that he is made what he is by the history of his fathers. Many of the customary ceremonials which make up the holiness of the Jewish home are purely history raised into tradition." [2]

The Jewish home is rooted in religious observance and derives its main strength from it. "Whenever we think of the Jewish home and its marvelous preservation throughout the millennia, we think of it as a little Holland, wrested from the waters of materialism, paganism, and animalism; and safeguarded against their deadly onslaught by certain dikes, constructed under Divine guidance by Israel's inspired engineers in the days of old. I would mention but a few of these dikes—*Kashrus,* and the moral discipline of the Jewish home; *Kiddush,* and home-religion; and *Kaddish* and all those beautiful symbols that sanctify birth and death, and link the generations in filial piety. If, whether through folly or disloyalty, any home or community levels these dikes, it is only a question of years before the waters of assimilation sweep over that home or that community, and it is no longer reckoned among the homes or communities of Israel. In a word, without a home-religion there is neither religion nor a true Jewish home for the Jew. "Except the Lord build the home, they toil in vain that build it." [3]

3. Sacred memories

In the traditional Jewish home father was the priest, mother the priestess, and the children, beings upon whose breath expended in the study of the Torah, the world existed. No wonder the traditional Jewish home generated and preserved sacred memories which kept the Jewish family so closely together. As in all sanctuaries, the Sabbath and Festival ceremonials played a major role in the Jewish home. The following two poems by a contemporary Jewish poet, Philip M. Raskin, captured the mood and the sentiment of the traditional home. The first describes the "Kindling the Sabbath Lights," on Friday at sundown:

> From memory's spring flows a vision to-night
> My mother is kindling and blessing the light;
>
> The light Queen Sabbath, the heavenly flame,
> That one day in seven quells hunger and shame.
>
> My mother is praying and screening her face,
> Too bashful to gaze at the Sabbath light's grace.
>
> She murmurs devoutly, "Almighty, be blessed,
> For sending Thy angel of joy and of rest.
>
> "And may as the candles of Sabbath divine
> The eyes of my son in Thy law ever shine."
>
> Of childhood, fair childhood, the years are long fled:
> Youth's candles are quenched, and my mother is dead.

And yet ev'ry Friday, when twilight arrives,
The face of my mother within me revives;

A prayer on her lips, "O Almighty, be blessed,
For sending us Sabbath, the angel of rest."

And some hidden feelings I cannot control
A Sabbath light kindles deep, deep in my soul.

The second poem describes the Seder, the beautiful, impressive and inspiring Passover Eve ritual-dinner of the Jewish home,—an emotional, aesthetic and spiritual link between parents and children:

Fair is the twilight,
And fragrant and still;
Little by little
The synagogues fill.

One by one kindle
The night's gleaming eyes;
Candles in windows
And stars in the skies.

Ended in *Shool* is
The service divine;
Seder is started
With legends and wine.

Father is blessing
The night of all nights;
All who are hungry
To feast he invites.

"All who are homeless
Yet masters shall be,
Slaves who are this year—
The next shall be free."

Children ask "questions,"
And father replies;
Playfully sparkle
The wine and the eyes.

Hymns of redemption
All merrily sing;
Queen is each mother,
Each father a king.

Midnight. The Seder
Is come to an end;
Guardian angels
From heaven descend.

Each one a message
Of liberty brings;
Scattering blessings
Of peace from her wings.

4. Need to re-create rites

If changed conditions deprive us of some of the old beautiful forms, we can and must create new ones.

"The beauty of the Jewish home resembles the ever-changing beauties of nature. God did not paint one sunset and hang it permanently in the sky. He paints a new sunset daily. Thus too do the beauties of the Jewish home pass through an endless cycle of repetition but not of exact duplication. Our mothers evolved new and beautiful settings and culinary masterpieces for the various days and seasons of the Jewish year. And just as today does not automatically inherit the brilliant array of yesterday's sunset, so the Jewish home of today does not and cannot automatically inherit the beauties of the Jewish home of yesterday. . . . It lies within the power of every Jewish woman, with the expenditure of just a little effort, to transform whatever habitation she may occupy into a Jewish Home Beautiful." [4]

5. Woman's responsibility

Today, more than ever, the responsibility for the Jewish character of the home rests upon the woman.

"Home is the grandest of all institutions, and the woman is the presiding genius of this institution. It is the duty of the Jewish woman to carry on the tradition of harmony and love that has always prevailed in Jewish home life. The creation of the home is work demanding infinite loving care and thought for the countless details for service. Each action or duty may by itself seem to be trivial, yet the result of the whole of the domestic service which woman can give means the creation of home. . . . Modern conditions have also deeded to the woman—for good or for evil—a considerable share of responsibility for the education of her children, both male and female. In former generations, while she gave much attention to the training of her daughters, the instruction of sons took place under the supervision of their fathers; the mother's duty was limited to their physical care. The father all too often has neither the time nor the knowledge to devote himself to the religious education of his children." [5]

6. Cooperation of home and school

"Formerly, the child absorbed most of its religious knowledge from the strength of the traditions and the life of the community around it. It lived in an atmosphere where the observance of Judaism was the rule, and where it picked up Jewish knowledge as it picked up its mother tongue. Today, a conscious, deliberate effort has been made to instill into the children Jewish teachings. It is on the woman that there devolves the responsibility for the maintenance of Jewish standards, and for the creation of a Jewish atmosphere from which the child shall learn emotionally the truths and duties of Judaism. It is usually the place of the mother to see that the children attend a religious school regularly and punctually. Yet the best school, giving a thorough course in Hebrew, Jewish history, Jewish traditions, and the principles and practices of Judaism, is building on sand unless there be Jewish spirit and Jewish observance in the home. If the foundation has been properly laid in the home, then the superstructure carefully built upon it by the combined efforts of the school, the synagogue, and the parents will endure. Then the brick upon brick of Jewish knowledge which is laid in the Talmud Torah will be cemented together by the mortar of the Judaism of the home." [6]

7. *Foundation of Jewish life*

Home is the primary place for Jewish life to take root.

"What native soil is to a plant, territory is to a civilization. Yet a tropical plant may be enabled to thrive in a northern climate by means of an enclosure within which the necessary conditions of temperature and sunshine are provided. Likewise, if Jewish life is to be cultivated outside its national homeland, it must be provided with a milieu congenial to its aims and modes of self-expression. The primary and indispensable *locus* of Jewish life is undoubtedly the home, where the child receives his first impressions, and where he obtains the basic layer of his cultural and spiritual life. It is there that the principal Jewish habits and Jewish values should be transmitted from one generation to the other. Therefore, whatever touches upon Judaism as a way of life has a bearing upon the Jewish home.

"Since Judaism is more than a religion or a religious philosophy, it cannot even begin to function in the individual as such. The family is the smallest social unit through which it can articulate itself. A philosophy, whether religious or secular, presupposes a high degree of individualization and detachment from the heat and turmoil of life; but it is only some form of associated life with all its accompanying vicissitudes that gives rise to a civilization. The minimum unit of a civilization consists of man, wife and child, for no person by himself can be a carrier of a civilization, which depends upon social interaction as well as upon transmission of cultural content from one generation to the next. From that standpoint, the problem of adjusting the Jewish home to social conditions of modern life is at the center of the problem of Judaism." [7]

8. *Cooperation of state and home*

"The question of momentous import, not only to Jews but to all western nations, is the question as to which civilization—the civic or the historic—shall have control of the home. In the effort to maintain the integrity of the family institution, the state has to depend largely upon the historic religious civilizations, upon Christianity for its Christian citizens, and upon Judaism for its Jewish citizens. The home will retain its wholesome influence provided the historic civilizations with their moral and religious values, will make a serious effort to re-enforce it by establishing better communal organization to act as the source of status and social standards, and by administering wise and systematic guidance in all questions that agitate the modern home." [8]

Questions for Discussion

1. What ceremonials in your parents' home do you recall with greatest pleasure? What ceremonials in *your* home will your child best remember?
2. What does the Sabbath Eve mean to your children? Are you satisfied that you are giving them the best in this respect?
3. How can we best create a beautiful and inspiring Jewish atmosphere in our homes?
4. What does the *Mezuzah* contain?

CHAPTER XXX

Sabbath: A People's Cultural Dynamo

1. For spiritual re-creativity

The civilization of a people is determined by how the people make a living. The culture of a people is determined by how the people live. The degree of the civilization of a people may be measured by its achievements in the means *by which* man lives. The culture of a people may be measured by its achievements in the things *for which* man lives. What a people does in its working hours will determine its civilization; what a people does in its leisure time will determine its culture.

The material means which a person uses in his labors is the product of the civilization around him. The spirit in which he approaches his work, the purpose of his work, what he does with his material achievements—these are determined by his culture. Hence the close relationship between work and leisure; the relationship between man's creativity and the leisure which affords man the opportunity to think and to regenerate his creative will and the power to be re-creative. The Jewish ideal of the Sabbath is, therefore, not an ideal of idleness but a day for spiritual and cultural re-creativity. It is not a negative day, a day of no work, but a day of spiritual growth. It is a day which is to give value and purpose to man's work on the other days. This relationship between work and leisure, between civilization and culture, is suggested in the Commandment on the Sabbath: "Six days shalt thou work and rest on the seventh."

2. A great contribution misunderstood

The Sabbath, the day of rest and of opportunity for social intercourse, discussion and cultural growth, is doubtless one of Israel's most precious contributions to the world. Yet so unique was the Jewish ideal that through the centuries the outside world failed fully to appreciate it. To the Greek and Roman intellectuals who doubtless never worked and who never could understand that servants were entitled to leisure, the Jewish Sabbath appeared so peculiar as to be an object of satire and ridicule.

"The attacks upon the Sabbath have not abated even in modern times. The day is still described by almost every modern writer in the most gloomy colors, and long lists are given of the minute observances connected with it, easily transgressed, which would necessarily make the Sabbath, instead of a day of rest, a day of sorrow and anxiety, almost worse than the Scotch Sunday, as depicted by continental writers. Even Hauserath—who is something more than a theologian, for he also wrote a history (History of the New Testament Times)—is unable to see the rabbinic Sabbath more than a day which is to be distinguished by a mere non-performance of the thirty-nine various sorts of work forbidden by the rabbis on Sabbaths. . . . Contrast this view with the prayer of R. Zadok, a younger contemporary of the Apostles, which runs thus:

'Through the love which Thou, O Lord our God, lovest Thy people Israel, and the mercy which Thou hast shown to the children of the covenant, Thou hast given unto us in love this great and holy seventh day.'

"This rabbi, clearly, regarded the Sabbath as a gift from heaven, an expression of the infinite love and mercy of God, which He manifested toward His beloved children. Thus the Sabbath is celebrated by the very people who observe it, in hundreds of hymns which would fill volumes, as a day of rest and joy, of pleasure and delight, a day in which man enjoys some presentiment of the pure bliss and happiness which are stored up for the righteous in the world to come, and to which such tender names were applied as the 'Queen Sabbath,' the 'Bride Sabbath,' and the 'holy, dearly beloved Sabbath.' Every founder of a religion declares the yoke which he is about to put on his followers easy, and the burden to be light; but, after all, the evidence of those who *did* bear the Sabbath yoke for thousands of years ought to pass for something." [1]

3. A priceless privilege

That the Jew considered the Sabbath not a burden but a priceless privilege is evidenced by the following dicta: Said the Holy One, blessed be He, to Moses: "I have a very fine gift in my treasure-house, and I desire to give it to Israel, go and notify them. The name of the gift is Sabbath." [2] The Sabbath balances all the other commandments.[3] "I am dark but beautiful"(Song of Songs, 1:5). This verse symbolizes Israel who may be dark all the week-days, but is beautiful on the Sabbath.[4] Said the Sabbath before the Holy One, blessed be He: "The other days of the week each has a mate (Sunday has Monday, Tuesday-Wednesday, Thursday-Friday), but I have no mate." Said the Lord: "I will give you a mate; the Congregation of Israel will be your mate." [5] It was in that union of Israel and the Sabbath that the ideals of Israel were born and the historic spirit of the Jew was preserved and nurtured. "More than Israel kept the Sabbath, the Sabbath kept Israel," Achad Ha'am so truly remarked.

The emperor asked R. Joshua: "How is it that your Sabbath food has so pleasant a fragrance?" The rabbi answered: "We possess a spice, named Sabbath, which we add to it, and that gives it its fragrance." The emperor asked for some of that spice, but the rabbi told him: "It only avails him who observes the Sabbath. It requires the traditional Sabbath atmosphere." [6]

4. Offered comfort and cheer

The following hymns and prayers indicate how the Jew felt on the Sabbath, what the day meant to him and what spirit and inspiration it gave him:

> I greet my love with wine and gladsome lay;
> Welcome, thrice welcome, joyous Seventh Day!

> Six slaves the week days are; I share
> With them a round of toil and care,
> Yet light the burdens seem, I bear
> For thy sweet sake, Sabbath, my love!

On First Day to the accustomed task
I go content, nor guerdon ask,
Save in thy smile, at length, to bask—
Day blest of God, Sabbath, my love!

Is Second Day dull, Third Day unbright?
Hide sun and stars from Fourth Day's sight?
What need I care, who have thy light,
Orb of my life, Sabbath, my love!

The Fifth Day, joyful tidings ring;
"The morrow shall thy freedom bring!"
At dawn a slave, at eve a king—
God's table waits, Sabbath, my love!

On Sixth Day does my cup o'erflow
What blissful rest the night shall know,
When, in thy arms, my toil and woe
Are all forgot, Sabbath, my love!

'Tis dusk. With sudden light distilled
From one sweet face, the world is filled;
The tumult of my heart is stilled—
For thou art come, Sabbath, my love!

Bring fruit and wine, and sing a gladsome lay,
Chant: "Come in peace, O blissful Seventh Day!" [7]

Come, my beloved, with chorusing praise,
Welcome the Sabbath Bride, Queen of the days.

Sabbath, to welcome thee, joyous we haste;
Fountain of blessing from ever thou wast,

For in God's planning, though fashioned the last—
Crown of His handiwork, chiefest of days. . . .

Come, my beloved, and banish all dread!
Welcome, the Sabbath Bride, Queen of the days. [8]

This day is for Israel light and rejoicing,
            A Sabbath of rest.

Thou badest us standing assembled at Sinai
That all the years through we should keep thy behest—
To set out a table full-laden, to honor
     A Sabbath of rest.

Treasure of heart for the broken people,
Gift of new soul for the souls distressed,
Soother of sighs for the prisoned spirit—
     A Sabbath of rest.

If I keep Thy command I inherit a kingdom,
If I treasure the Sabbath I bring Thee the best—
The noblest of offerings, the sweetest of incense
     A Sabbath of rest.[9]

The reward for the observance of the Sabbath is the opportunity to observe this joyous day again:

"Two angels accompany the Jew from the synagogue on Sabbath eve. One is the good angel and the other is the angel of evil. As they enter the home and find the table set, the candles bright and the Sabbath spirit permeating the house, the angel of good says: 'May next week be like this.' And the angel of evil says, 'Amen.' But if no trace of the Sabbath is found in the home, then the angel of evil says: 'May next week be like this.' And the good angel must say, 'Amen.'"[10]

5. Generated beauty and strength

"The Sabbath made the Jewish home beautiful. On this day the persecuted Jew became a prince, sovereign of his brood. With an *Oreah,* a guest, the Jew returns from the Synagogue on the eve of the Sabbath to greet the *Sabbath Bride.* His home, though lacking in worldly splendor, is sanctified by the mellow glow of the Sabbath candles. On a table, decked in a snowy cloth, lie two golden-brown loaves of Sabbath bread, symbolic of the two-fold commandment to 'remember the Sabbath day and keep it holy.' The two golden loaves remind him also of the double portion of manna that our ancestors received for the Sabbath when they wandered in the wilderness. As the Jew lifts his Kiddush cup, his glistening table is a festive board. With wife and children gathered about him, he welcomes the Sabbath day. Joy, warmth, hospitality, peace—these make his Jewish home beautiful." [11]

"The Jew was compensated for the hostility and contempt in the outer world by the sympathy, understanding and help he found in his Jewish world. . . . A well-known poem by Heine depicts what the Sabbath did for the Jew who, during the week, went about peddling his wares among the Gentiles, and who returned for the Sabbath to his home in the ghetto. It was the Sabbath, the holy day which God had given to His people . . . that performed the miracle of transforming the Jew from a dog into a prince. This transformation came about through his contact with his people and participation in their life. It was thus that he received a foretaste of the salvation for which he prayed on the Sabbath, 'May the All-merciful let us inherit the day which shall be wholly a Sabbath and rest in the life everlasting.' " [12]

"The Sabbath is, first of all, a day of rest, a day to be marked by the cessation of the weekly round of work. No one can be toiling uninterruptedly day after day and year after year without impairing sooner or later his powers of body and mind. . . . But the preservation of the bodily health was only part of the purpose of the Sabbath. . . . The enforced rest of the Sabbath was to afford the Jew an opportunity for that communion with his higher self which the toilsome week denied him. . . . And so the Sabbath was to be hallowed by a twofold consecration. It was to be devoted, in the first place, to that duty of safeguarding the welfare of the body which Judaism has always held sacred. And it was further to be dedicated to that better part of man which constitutes his true, his real self." [13]

On the Sabbath a *Neshamah Yetherah,* an "added soul" is given to man, an increased capacity for lofty thoughts and aspirations.[14] This "added soul" comes down from heaven each week and brings with it a taste of the spiritual bliss of heaven. It is scented with the perfume of the *Gan Eden,* and as it reaches earth, sorrow and sadness depart and peace and joy reign supreme.[15]

6. *Its moral uplift*

"No one has kept the Sabbath holy who has not devoted some part of it to religious exercises—to prayer, to serious reading and meditation, to solemn self-communion. But no one has kept it holy who has not learned from it a deeper respect for his work, however humble it may be. Moreover, the Sabbath, with its command to us to rest, is a rebuke to our avarice, our sordidness, our selfishness. It reminds us that we live for higher things than gain. 'There are higher objects in life than success.' The Sabbath, with its exhortation to the worship of God and the doing of kindly deeds, reminds us week by week of these higher objects. It prevents us from reducing our life to the level of a machine. . . . To dedicate one day a week to rest and to God, this is the prerogative and privilege of man alone. It is an ordinance which we may rightly call Divine." [16]

7. No "blue" Sabbath

Noticing a Jew who appeared melancholy on the Sabbath, the Rabbi of Ger, said to him: "The Sabbath is known to offer hospitality to guests. If the New Moon occurs on the Sabbath, she offers to it portions of the prayers; to the Intermediate Festivals she yields the *Musaph;* to the Festivals and to *Yom Kippur* she yields the entire service. There is one guest, however, to which the Sabbath will not grant admittance, namely, the Fast of the Ninth of Ab. The Sabbath is eager for joy, but she has no place for sadness." [17]

8. In the home and the synagogue today

What of the Sabbath today? "In the last instance, not what the Jew will refrain from doing will determine the spiritual influence of the Sabbath, but the affirmative conduct which the observance of the Sabbath will elicit from him. The Sabbath must make itself felt in the home. Only there can its observance be made attractive enough to impel the Jew to effort and sacrifice in its behalf. . . . During the Sabbath day, the home should have a distinct Sabbath atmosphere. How to spend the day outside the home should constitute the problem for the synagogue, or neighborhood center, which should provide the facilities for spending the day with physical and spiritual advantage. . . . Apart from the spiritual value which attaches to the experience of merging oneself with a body of people who unite for self-expression in worship, Jewish life must offer some visible outlet for folk spirit and self-expression; and nothing is so essential for that purpose as public worship. Sabbaths and festivals will not be celebrated in the home in a manner that will unite the Jew to his people unless public worship supplies the incentive." [18]

Questions for Discussion

1. Can you conceive of an inspiring Jewish life without a synagogue, and of a synagogue without a Sabbath?
2. Does economic pressure alone account for the extent of the popular departure from the traditional Sabbath observance?
3. How can the Sabbath spirit be regenerated in the home?
4. What role can the synagogue play in the regeneration of the Sabbath spirit?
5. What effect does the recitation of the *Kiddush* have on the Sabbath spirit in the home?
6. Are any Jewish public offices in your community open on the Sabbath? If so, what is your attitude toward this practice?
7. Can we long remain a cultured people without a Sabbath?

CHAPTER XXXI

A Chosen People

1. Biblical views

"Now the Lord said unto Abram: '. . . I will make of thee a great nation, and I will bless thee, and make thy name great; and be thou a blessing. And I will bless them that bless thee, and him that curseth thee will I curse; and in thee shall all the races of the earth be blessed.' " [1]

"I have chosen him that he may charge his sons and his household after him to follow the directions of the eternal by doing what is good and right." [2]

"What are you more than the Ethiopians, Oh Israelites? the Eternal asks. I brought up Israel from Egypt? Yes, and the Philistines from Crete, from Kir the Aramaeans." [3]

"Thus said God the Lord: '. . . I the Lord have called thee in righteousness and have taken hold of thine hand, and kept thee, and set thee for a covenant of the people, for a light unto the nations; to open the blind eyes, to bring out the prisoners from the dungeon, and them that sit in darkness out of the prison house.' " [4]

2. Conscious of group responsibility

The above biblical texts sum up the Jewish ideal of a Chosen People. A people is chosen not because of any racial superiority; there is no such thing. All men are the children of Adam; all are created in God's image —Jew and Gentile, Hebrew, Ethiopian, Philistine or Aramaean. A people is chosen when it has the will to live in a way which would express God's spirit on earth. A people is chosen when it measures its growth by moral and spiritual and not by material and geographic standards. A people is chosen when it is held together by spirit and not by might. A people is chosen when its highest ideal is not to get as much as possible from the world but to contribute of its best to the world, when it endeavors to live as the "Servant of the Lord"—"a blessing unto the nations." Israel did not always live up to this position. But it is a historic fact that Israel, of all the peoples, always considered itself a candidate for such a position. When one is a candidate one is often elected; when one is not a candidate, one can hardly be elected.

3. No special privileges

Neither the prophets nor the rabbis ever claimed any special privileges for Israel as a Chosen People. On the contrary, instead of getting any material advantages from this choice, Israel bears a heavier responsibility and a greater liability to discipline and punishment. "Because God loved Israel He multiplied suffering for him." [5] "Three precious gifts did the Holy One, blessed be He, bestow upon Israel, and all of them He gave only through Israel's suffering, *viz.*, the Torah, the Land of Israel, and the World to Come." [6]

4. Acceptance of responsibility

An ancient rabbinic legend stresses the point that it was not God's arbitrary will to choose Israel but rather that it was Israel's will to choose God: Before God gave Israel the Torah, He approached every tribe and nation, and offered them the Torah. . . . He went to the children of Esau and said, "Will you accept the Torah?" They asked, "What is written therein?" He answered them, "Thou shalt not kill." They said: "Wilt Thou perchance take from us the blessing with which our father Esau was blessed? For he was blessed with the words, 'By the sword shalt thou live.' We do not want to accept the Torah." Thereupon He went to the children of Lot and offered them the Torah. "What is written therein?" they asked. He told them, "Thou shalt not commit adultery." They said: "From unchastity do we spring; we do not want to accept the Torah." Ishmael refused to accept the Torah because it contains "Thow shalt not steal." Ishmael's ideal was "His hand shall be against every man." God then went to all the other nations, who likewise rejected the Torah, saying: "We cannot give up the law of our fathers, we do not want the Torah." He then cáme to the Israelites and offered them the Torah. "What is written therein?" they asked. He answered, "Six hundred and thirteen commandments." They said: "All that the Lord has spoken we will do and obey." They maintained that they acted in accordance with the Commandments before they were revealed, and that they discerned in the Commandments the traditional ideals of their patriarchs.[7]

5. The international heart

The election of Israel means that Israel is to the nations what the heart is to the rest of the body. The heart suffers most for it reacts to the ills of all parts of the body. But the heart has the power to throw off the impurities and to send life-giving forces to the body. A similar role is enacted by Israel among the nations.[8]

6. Dedicated to an ideal and a mission

Election of Israel means that Israel is a people dedicated to the teaching of the unity of God: Before Abraham men erred by believing that they were worshiping God when they worshiped and built altars in honor of the stars and constellations which He created. . . . But Abraham conceived that the One God was the Prime Cause and Direct Ruler of the universe. . . . Abraham endeavored to teach this doctrine of God to his generation. He taught it to Isaac, who transmitted it to Jacob, who taught it to all of his children. This doctrine grew and spread among Jacob's children and among all who joined with them and thus there developed in the world a people with a knowledge of God.[9]

Cruelty and arrogance are common among idol worshipers. But Israel, the seed of Abraham, imbued with God's Torah and His just laws and statutes, is commanded to imitate Him and be merciful to all.[10]

Our patriarchs, Abraham, Isaac and Jacob, believed in the Lord God. They wandered not from His right paths and walked before Him. In the hearts of their children too they implanted pure sentiments and noble thoughts, free of all pagan conceptions. They taught them to love God and observe His Commandments. When the Lord saw their fine actions and what Abraham taught his children, He made an eternal covenant with him that his children should become a chosen people and a kingdom of priests—a kingdom whose laws, regulations and ordinances as well as its history should be a lesson to all their neighbors regarding the right path to follow. . . . These lessons are not to be abstract principles and philosophic symbols but should consist in actual examples of daily living. . . . Abstract theologies lead to idolatry and create barriers between man and man. But in the life and daily example of a true scholar and saint one has theory and practice, law and life, creed and deed combined. This was characteristic of Israel's ideal of election.[11]

7. Not exclusive

It must be noted that this doctrine of election—and it is difficult to see how any revealed religion can dispense with it—was not quite of so exclusive a nature as is commonly imagined. For it is only the privilege of the first-born which the rabbis claim for Israel, that they are the first in God's kingdom, not to the exclusion of other nations. A God "Who had faith in the world when He created it," who mourned over its moral decay, which compelled Him to punish it with the deluge, as a father mourns over the death of his son, and who, but for their sins, longed to make His abode among its inhabitants, is not to be supposed to have entirely given up all relations with the great majority of mankind, or to have ceased to take any concern in their well-being.[12]

Interesting is the rabbinic comment on the verse "Hear, O Israel, the Lord is our God, the Lord is One": He is *our* God by making His name particularly attached to us (revealed through us); but He is also the One God of *all* mankind. He is *our* God in this world, He will be the only God in the world to come.[13] . . . In this world men, through the insinuations of the evil inclination, have divided themselves into various tongues, but in the world of the future they will agree with one consent to call only on His name.[14] . . . Thus the *Shema* not only contains a metaphysical statement (about the unity of God), but expresses a hope and belief . . . in the ultimate universal kingdom of God.[15] The advancement of the kingdom of God on earth *through* Israel but not *for*

Israel alone but for all mankind, this is Israel's idea of a Chosen People. "The election of Israel does not imply the rejection of mankind." [16]

8. *"The servant of the Lord"*

The real purpose of the election and mission of Israel was announced by the great prophet of the Exile when he called Israel the "servant of the Lord," who has been formed from his mother's bosom . . . to be a harbinger of light and a bond of union among the nations, the witness of God, the proclaimer of His truth and righteousness throughout the world. . . . The belief in the election of Israel rests on the conviction that the Jewish people has a certain superiority over other peoples in being especially qualified to be the messenger and champion of religious truth. In one sense this prerogative takes into account every people which has contributed something unique to any department of human power or knowledge, and therein has served others as pattern and guide. From the broader standpoint, all great historic peoples appear as though appointed by divine providence for their special cultural tasks, in which others can at most emulate them without achieving their greatness. Yet we cannot speak in quite the same way of the election of the Greeks and Romans or of the nations of remote antiquity for mastery in art and science, or for skill in jurisprudence and statecraft. The fact is that these nations were never fully conscious that they had a historic or providential destiny to influence mankind in this special direction. Israel alone was self-conscious, realizing its task as harbinger and defender of its religious truth as soon as it entered into its possession. Its election, therefore, does not imply presumption, but rather a great responsibility. [17]

9. *The discipline of the Torah*

The traditional prayer book constantly refers to the special election of Israel, but in every case the implication is not to any material gains but to the privilege of guidance and discipline of the Torah. Thus: "With everlasting love Thou hast loved the house of Israel, Thy people; a Torah and commandments, statutes and judgments hast Thou taught us." [18]

Again "Blessed art Thou, O Lord our God, King of the universe, who hast chosen us from all nations and given us Thy Torah. Blessed art Thou, O Lord, who givest the Torah." [19]

"If the Jews regarded themselves as more qualified for salvation than the rest of mankind, it was not because they believed that they possessed intrinsically superior mental and moral traits. The predominant teaching has been that the Jewish people owed the prerogative of salvation entirely to the particular way of life to which it had dedicated itself. In Jewish tradition that particular way of life is regarded as set forth in the Torah. The term "Torah" not only refers to the particular corpus of writings which include the Bible and the rabbinic literature, but also assigns a position of pre-eminence and authority to these writings. Upon them the Jewish consciousness has been riveted for the last two millennia. . . . There can be nothing more paradoxical than a Torah-less Judaism. A Jewish life whose entire stream of consciousness from one end of the year to the next does not receive a single idea or impression directly from the Jewish writings which embody the great Jewish tradition would indeed be anomalous. . . . So long as there is found any room in the contemporary scene for Jewish life, the knowledge of Torah must figure in it, or that life will be anything but Jewish. . . . But of even greater importance for the reordering of Jewish life than the study of the sacred writings, is the fostering of a mode of life that will be animated by whatever in the traditional attitude toward the Torah is of incontestable worth. . . . Torah should mean to the Jew nothing less than a civilization which enables the individual to effect affirmative and creative adjustments in his living relationships with reality. Any partial conception of Torah is false to the forces that have made for Judaism's development and survival. But to the Jew in the diaspora it must, in addition, spell the duty of beholding in the non-Jewish civilization in which he lives a potential instrument of salvation. He must help to render that civilization capable of enhancing human life as the Torah enhanced the life of Israel. If, like the Torah, it is to be worthy of fervent devotion, those whose lives it fashions must be convinced of its intrinsic. righteousness." [20]

In other words, in addition to his efforts to make Israel worthy of the full implications of a Chosen People, it is the duty of the Jew, because of his Jewish traditions, to make his full contribution to help the people in whose midst he lives and whose civilization he shares, become a Chosen People in its finest and noblest sense.

Questions for Discussion

1. What effect did our historic conception of a Chosen People have upon Jewish survival?
2. Does our position as free citizens require that we give up this conception of a Chosen People?
3. What would happen to humanity if all peoples considered themselves chosen in the Jewish historic sense?
4. What should be the behavior of a Jew who considers himself a member of the Chosen People as defined by the prophets and rabbis?

CHAPTER XXXII

Jew and Non-Jew

1. The pious of all nations

As was shown in the previous chapter, the election of the Jew does not imply the rejection of the non-Jew.

Said the rabbis: "The pious of all the nations of the world have a share in the world to come." [1]

"Even a Gentile who obeys the Torah is the equal of the High Priest. It is not stated, 'Open the gates that priests or Levites or Israelites may enter,' but 'Open the gates that a righteous *Goy,* i.e., Nation—any righteous nation—may enter' (Is. 26:2). Again, it is not stated, 'This is the gate of the Lord, priests or Levites or Israelites shall enter into it.' . . . It is not stated, 'Do good, O Lord, to the priests or Levites or Israelites,' but 'unto the good' (Ps. 125:4). Hence anyone—Jew or non-Jew—who obeys the Torah is the equal of the High Priest." [2]

2. No isolationism

The Jew always considered himself part of the larger humanity, and he prayed for the welfare of all. "On the Feast of Tabernacles, seventy bullocks were offered on behalf of the seventy nations." [3] Solomon's prayer at the dedication of the Temple proclaimed it a house of worship for all peoples: "As for the alien, who does not belong to Thy people Israel but who came from a distant land for Thy sake . . . when he comes and turns in prayer toward this Temple, then do Thou listen in Thy home, in heaven, and do all that the alien asks of Thee, so that all nations of the world may learn what Thou art, learning to revere Thee, like Thy people Israel." [4]

3. No monopoly on salvation

The Jew never claimed to have a monopoly on God or salvation. "Whether Gentile or Israelite, whether man or woman, whether freeman or slave, in accord with his personal worth does the Holy Spirit rest upon him." [5] "Every human being who has developed the understanding to stand before God, to serve Him in knowledge and walk uprightly as God made him to do, such an individual is sanctified manifold, and the Lord will be his portion and his heritage forever." [6]

Neither does the Jew claim to have a monopoly on culture and wisdom. "The beauty of Japhet may rest in the tents of Shem." [7] The rabbis applied it to the value of introducing the worthwhile cultural achievements of the world in general into Jewish life. Many of the sages of the ancient peoples learned to speculate and reason in matters of basic faith. We may learn from them. [8] The rabbis greatly respected the learned of all peoples, and even ordained that a Jew should pronounce a blessing of thanksgiving when meeting a scholar whether he be Jew or non-Jew. If the scholar is a Jew the blessing is, "Blessed art Thou, O Lord, our God, King of the universe, Who hast given of Thy wisdom to them that fear Thee"; if a Gentile, the blessing is, "Blessed Art Thou, O Lord, our God, King of the universe, Who hast given of Thy wisdom to a human being." [9] Of course this formula goes back to the days when the Gentiles were pagans. Today, even this distinction may not apply.

4. "All men are born equal"

The basic fact to be remembered in the relationship between Jew and non-Jew is that Judaism teaches clearly and explicitly the unity of the human race. Since, according to the biblical creation story, the first pair was created by direct command, it follows that all men share in a noble and holy origin, a doctrine which lays the foundation for the ideal of mutual respect and esteem among men. The Mosaic law made no distinction in the enjoyment of civil and political rights between the Israelite and the non-Israelite dwelling in the land. As for the *Ger,* the alien who came to settle permanently in the land of Israel, the Bible ordains over and over again not only equal but kind and considerate treatment; "One manner of law shall be for you, for the alien as for the native-born, for I am the Lord, your God" (Lev. 24:22). "And if an alien sojourn with thee in your land, ye shall not vex him. As one native-born among you shall be the alien that sojourneth with you, and thou shalt love him as thyself, for ye were strangers in the land of Egypt; I am the Lord your God" (Lev. 19:33 f.).

5. A world at peace

Inspired by the ideal of the unity of the human family as presented in the Pentateuch, the prophets of Israel looked forward to a time when war, that curse of humanity in all ages, will cease. Isaiah and Micah picture such a time:

"And He shall judge between the nations, and shall decide for many peoples; and they shall beat their swords into plowshares, and their spears into pruning hooks; nation shall not lift up sword against nation, and they shall not learn war anymore." [10]

6. All God's children

The Hebrew prophets mourned over the afflictions of other peoples as they did over Israel's. Thus, Jeremiah, the classic mourner for Zion, lamented also for Moab. "Therefore my heart moaneth for Moab like flutes, and my heart moaneth like flutes for the men of Kir-Heresh" (Jer. 48:36). All peoples were to the Hebrew prophets God's children. Isaiah said, "Blessed be My people Egypt, My handiwork Assyria, and My inheritance Israel" (19:24). The general spirit of biblical Judaism, far from being a narrow tribal cult, self-centered and hostile, or, at best, unsympathetic in its attitude toward non-Jews, was on the contrary truly universal and broadly humanitarian, considering all human beings children of the One Heavenly Father, and sincerely desirous of promoting the spiritual, ethical, and material welfare of all mankind.[11]

7. God's justice international

Before the Japanese attack on Pearl Harbor, most of our so-called liberals were isolationists. They were the men who considered the Old Testament ideals tribal. Yet what is the lesson of the book of Jonah?

Jonah, a citizen of Judaea, was sent to protest against the behavior of a foreign nation, Assyria. The Bible condemns him for trying to avoid this responsibility. Yet if Jonah were a "liberal" before Pearl Harbor, he might have said that it was not *right* for a citizen of one country to interfere with the internal affairs of another country! But the author of Jonah, as a Jew, considered the welfare of all, the responsibility of each.

8. Tolerance and neighborliness

Post-biblical Judaism carried on the universal spirit of the Bible. A few Talmudic statements will illustrate this fact: "Gentiles living outside of Palestine are not to be considered willful idolators, even though they maintain idolatrous worship, but merely as continuing the traditional customs of their ancestors." [12] In other words they are not to be blamed for not seeing nobler examples to follow. Rabbi Judah and Raba, two eminent sages, sent presents to their Gentile friends on their holiday, explaining that they did not consider them idolators.[13] "It is incumbent upon the Jew to make no distinction in charitable assistance between Jew and non-Jew but to help all the poor and the sick." [14]

9. An inspiring legend

When the Egyptian pursuers of Israel were drowning in the Red Sea, an old rabbinic legend relates, the angels sought to sing a song of triumph. But the Holy One, blessed be He, rebuked them and said, "My creatures are drowning in the sea and would ye sing a song!" [15] A legend, to be sure! But a legend conceived by a Jewish mind, and transmitted as sacred doctrine to generations of Jews to the present day. The persecutors of Israel deserved their punishment, but in the hour of their suffering their evil deeds must be forgotten and compassion must take the place of the spirit of revenge.

10. Respecting the faith of others

During the Middle Ages, many of the Jewish teachers were thoroughly acquainted with the non-Jewish culture of their time. Their teachings in reference to the relations between Jews and Gentiles, while based on Jewish tradition, show liberality and understanding of the non-Jewish viewpoint. Maimonides, the greatest Jewish thinker of the Middle Ages, who had himself, in his youth, suffered sadly from Mohammedan fanaticism, was most liberal in his attitude toward non-Jews and non-Jewish religions. In his great work, *Yad ha-Hazakah,* an encyclopaedic code of Judaism (which has received a place of authority in the synagogue), he expresses himself thus on the religious status of the non-Jew: "Our master Moses, blessed be his memory, made the Law and the commandments incumbent only 'upon Israel . . . and upon those of the other nations who wish to become converts. . . . But whoever does not wish to accept the Torah but accepts the commandments of the children of Noah and fulfills them sincerely, is accounted one of the pious of the Gentiles and shall have a portion in the world to come." [16] The seven commandments of the children of Noah are: the practice of equity, prohibition against blaspheming the Name, idolatry, immorality, bloodshed, robbery, and devouring a limb torn from a live animal.[17]

Among later rabbinic decisions we find: The Talmudic laws concerning heathens do not apply to Christians and Mohammedans.[18] The name of Israel applies to all righteous men, and may, therefore, be applied to the righteous of all peoples.[19] This reminds one of the remark of Nathan to the Crusader in Lessing's "Nathan the Wise": "That which makes me a Christian to you, makes you a Jew to me." One of the great rabbinic zealots of the 18th century, states that the founder of Christianity was a benefactor of humanity in two ways. In the first place, he laid stress on the influence and importance of Torah; and, in the second place, he led heathens away from idol worship and insisted on their adopting morality.[20]

Writing to a non-Jewish friend, Moses Mendelssohn said: "Your question, why I do not try to make converts, has, I must say, somewhat surprised me. The duty to proselytise springs clearly from the idea that outside a certain belief there is no salvation. I, as a Jew, am not bound to accept that dogma, because, according to the teachings of the rabbis, *the righteous of all nations shall have a part in the rewards of the future world.* Your motive, therefore, is foreign to me; nay, as a Jew, I am not allowed publicly to attack any religion which is sound in its moral teachings." [21]

11. Each according to his convictions

One will recall the beautiful parable of the Three Rings quoted in Lessing's "Nathan the Wise." The application of the parable is to the three religions—Christianity, Mohammedanism, and Judaism—and the lesson is that the adherents of each should believe that their faith is the true one and, inspired by that faith, should live together in friendship and mutual tolerance. A Jewish scholar of our day took exception to the implication of this parable. Since only one of the rings is genuine and the other two necessarily false, the implication is that, of the three great religions of the world, one is the true faith and the other two are false, based on fraud and deception. Intrinsically there is no such thing as a false religion. All religions have the same fundamental purpose; to bring man into communion with the Deity and to set up an ethical rule of life. The particular form of religion to which a man adheres is determined by his birth and the history of his people. It is the manner in which the religious impulse realized itself in him; and to him, therefore, it is a true religion.[22]

12. The ideals and tasks we share

"Science has brought material comforts, but not happiness. It has removed the barriers of space but has not brought nations together. . . . The products of science are now ravaging the face of the world a thousand times more cruelly than war ever ravaged it before. If ever the message of religion was needed, its moral inspiration, its exhortation to Faith, its injunctions to Justice and Mercy, its definition of values for the guidance of men and nations, it is needed today. . . . Religion says that the individual is something more than a totalitarianized grain of sand to be kicked and trampled on at the will of a dictator, and that his soul and his personality are inviolable. It says that the individual has rights divinely guaranteed which not even the State or its rulers can trespass. . . . Religion says that the most important and the most sacred relationship in life, more sacred than the relationship between the subject and the State is the eternal triangle of father, mother, and child. Religion says that . . . no nation is so privileged as to be beyond the bar of eternal justice. . . . The spokesmen who spoke in the name of Religion were not popular in high places. . . . Somehow it (Religion) survived both its scheming foes and its over-solicitous friends and it is here today as the Jewish-Christian tradition. . . . We are witnessing a resurgence of paganism. . . . What is needed is a resurgence of Religion. . . . This is the broad task incumbent upon Jew and Christian. The present crisis in human affairs has drawn them together more closely than they have been for centuries. Let each seek nourishment in the rich, spiritual matrix of his own religious tradition. Let the Christian repair to his altar, let the Jew repair to his altar, consecrated by the Prophets and Sages, the Psalmists and Saints. We have too much to do together to permit our forces to be divided. Together we must seek, by the exercise of our living creeds to impress upon our world of chaos and darkness, the primordial command, 'Let there be light.' " [23]

Questions for Discussion

1. If our religion is right must we therefore assume that all other religions are wrong?
2. Is religious uniformity conducive to spiritual growth?
3. What do Jews and Christians have in common in their basic faiths?

CHAPTER XXXIII

Nationalism

1. A nation founded on Torah

The Eternal said to Abram, "Leave thy country, leave thy kindred, leave thy father's house, for a land that I will show thee; I will make a great nation of thee, and I will bless thee and make thy name great; and in thee shall the families of the earth be blessed" (Gen. 12: 1–3).

This verse introduces Israel in its historic role as a nation. But we must note that Israel is not a nation in the common sense of the word. To the rabbis, at least, it is not a nation by virtue of race or of certain political combinations. As Saadya Gaon expressed it, "Because our nation is only a nation by reason of Torah." [1] "The brutal Torah-less nationalism promulgated in certain quarters, would have been to the rabbis just as hateful as the suicidal Torah-less universalism preached in other quarters. And if we could imagine for a moment Israel giving up its allegiance to God, its Torah and its divine institutions, the rabbis would be the first to sign its death-warrant as a nation." [2]

The most sublime expressions of Jewish nationalism are to be found in the Bible and the Prayer Book. Here is a specimen of the latter: "O Guardian of an only nation, guard the remnant of an only nation, and suffer not an only nation to perish, who proclaim the unity of Thy name, saying 'The Lord our God, the Lord is One.' " But the nationalism of the purely secular kind as taught by certain philosophers and historians within the last two generations leading to the excesses which we are witnessing now all over the world had better be relegated to the lecture platform. Jewish nationalism can best be interpreted only in the light of Jewish history and pure Jewish thought. Moreover, the world is sure to combine against the fanaticism of modern chauvinism just as it did

combine in the eighteenth century against religious fanaticism. And
Judaism should ponder deeply before it entirely identifies itself with this
sort of exaggerated secular nationalism. An ancient Jewish moralist had
a maxim: "If you are in the humor of praising, praise God; and if you
are in the frame of mind of blaming, blame yourself." And I am certain
that the time has come when this maxim will be applied as much to
whole groups of humanity as to individuals. Jewish nationalism is holy
to the Lord, and any attempt to sever it from the historical Jewish ideals
attached to the biblical terms "God's People," or "Holy Nation," will
fail in the end.[3]

2. Need for universal purpose

"To assume that it is possible for the Jews to maintain their nationhood without believing that there is something in it of universal significance is to reckon without human nature. Jewish nationalists, who
contend that the sense of nationhood requires no justification in any
universal purpose, are correct only as far as the challenging outsider is
concerned. To be sure, one cannot change one's grandmother, but one's
beliefs do affect one's grandchildren. If they are to be born into a Jewish nation, that nationhood must constitute a high moral asset. Jews
must therefore find a meaning in their status as a nation, or failing this,
must construct one that will justify the effort and struggle involved in
upholding that status. Such a meaning would be the equivalent of the
traditional belief in Israel's divine election, and, therefore, the functional
revaluation of that belief." [4]

"When the Jews affirmed that they were God's chosen nation, their
claim was tantamount to the assertion that they alone constituted a nation. They meant to emphasize their belief that all the other peoples,
including the most powerful, were not really nations. This interpretation of the doctrine of election rests not only on the words of an ancient
singer in Israel who said: 'Thou art the One (God) and Thy Name is
One: and who is there like Thy people, the one nation in the world?'
It rests upon the entire outlook of ancient man to whom godhood was
but a higher form of kinghood. . . . Therefore, when the Jews arrived
at the belief that the gods of the other nations were nonentities, they

concluded that the other nations were not nations in the true sense of the term. . . . Though there may be a certain crude 'sacred egoism' in this doctrine, its implications are important. It implies not only a tribute to nationhood as the ideal arrangement under which human beings can achieve their highest good, but also the consciousness of a standard which nationhood must attain to fulfill its function. Throughout rabbinic literature it is assumed that the Torah constituted the principal instrument which confers nationhood upon the Jews. . . . As a covenant, the Torah is the symbol, representing the truth that a nation becomes such, not through the accident of common ancestry or physical propinquity, but through the consent of those who constitute it to live together and to make their common past the inspiration for a common future. The general will that speaks in such consent is the spiritual bond which unites the members of a nation. Any people that develops a general will of that kind has acquired a collective personality and an inalienable right to existence, limited only by the right to existence of similar groups which have developed a general and articulated will of their own. . . . The Torah emphasizes the general truth that a nation is not a fighting unit but a cultural group, united not by instincts that keep together wolf-packs for purposes of offense and defense, but by the urge to develop those human differentiae and potentialities which only collective life can bring forth." [5]

3. The State an agency for universal purpose

"The prophets of Israel, these revolutionists, *par excellence,* fully and solicitously acknowledge all that is historical in the life of the nation, all that has matured in the course of national existence, and has proved its efficacy and vitality. It is a remarkable fact, by no means sufficiently appreciated, that the prophets of Israel, who frequently were the irreconcilable enemies of the powers that be, . . . never tried to overthrow the government, or to undermine the constitution of their country. . . . The prophets knew full well that a nation without a State is like a spirit without a body, that a nation, like any other organism, cannot perform its functions when dissected into atoms. But while fully recognizing the necessity of the State and all the forces attached to it, they endeavored to infuse into it a new soul, to assign to it a new function. . . . The State in itself is not the 'glory of Jacob,' the expression of Israel's superiority, it is merely the human agency for carrying into effect the true superiority of Israel—the religious, or social, or ethical ideal." [6]

4. Zion a free spiritual center

"Twenty-five centuries have passed since the political ideal of the prophets was put to the test in the Babylonian captivity and carried to victory by the returned exiles on the reconquered mount of Zion. And now their late descendants, the sons of the *Galuth,* are confronted by similar dangers and difficulties. . . . The wheel of history has brought on the scene two new factions which our ancestors knew not. It has been left to our age of science and cold materialism to evolve a conception of Israel which detaches it from its soil and turns it into a spirit without a body. On the other hand, even those who continue to hope look upon Zion as the material center of our people, as its refuge from poverty and distress, and the glorious embodiment of its economic and political grandeur. The former hope to preserve the Jewish spirit without Zion, the latter would save Zion even without the Jewish spirit. But those of us who still cherish the memory of the prophets and pin their faith to their ideals, see in Zion above all the consummation of our *spiritual* strivings. To them Zion does not spell the great numbers and vast territories. . . . To them Zion is dear as the *spiritual* center of our people, where, independent of numbers and dimensions, the Jewish *spirit* can develop free and unhampered, where the 'holy remnant,' conscious of its mission, lives as a model and a blessing to the rest of Israel and mankind, where the ancient ideal is realized in a modern form: 'For out of Zion shall go forth the Law, and the word of the Lord from Jerusalem.' " [7]

Questions for Discussion

1. Is there anything distinctive about Jewish nationalism?
2. Is religion an integral part of Jewish nationalism?
3. Can the Jewish nation survive without Torah?

4. What are the moral possibilities of nationalism?
5. Would you abolish all national groups?
6. Would there be wars if we abolished all national divisions?
7. Is the present war a war between nations or ideologies?

CHAPTER XXXIV

The Homeland

1. Religious and historic bond

"Now the Lord has said unto Abram, 'Get thee out of thy country . . . unto the land that I will show thee.' . . . And they came unto the land of Canaan. . . . And the Lord said: 'Unto thy seed will I give this land' " (Gen. 12).

From the days of Abraham to modern times, Jewish history is intimately tied up with the Land of Canaan, with Palestine, with *Eretz Yisroel*. We see Israel only on the way to Palestine, in Palestine, or praying for its restoration and constantly endeavoring to re-settle it. From Abraham to Weizmann, Palestine is established as the land of Jewish promise and hope.

The promise made to Abraham is repeated to Isaac and confirmed to Jacob. Joseph's last charge, when he is dying in Egypt, is that his bones shall be taken up from Egypt and brought back to the land which God swore to Abraham, to Isaac and to Jacob. . . . What follows in Israel's story is the long but successful struggle to attain an increasingly strong hold on the land. . . . Then and only then was Jewish life first given the opportunity to develop its own free, characteristic contributions to mankind's social, moral and spiritual wealth. . . . Judaism in its all-engrossing entirety is possible only in the land of the Jews. . . . By the waters of Babylon the exiled Jews truly said: "How shall we sing the Lord's song in a foreign land?" [1]

It was there that they took the historic oath: "If I forget thee, O Jerusalem, let my right hand forget her cunning. Let my tongue cleave to the roof of my mouth, if I remember thee not, if I set not Jerusalem above my chiefest joy." This oath the Jews sacredly kept right down to our own generation—a unique and glorious example of a people's loyalty to a land and to a covenant.

2. *Continuity of Jewish occupation*

"When the Lord brought back 'those that returned to Zion,' the Jewish community was reestablished in Palestine, and the hope of Jewish survival was renewed. During the following centuries, Jewish life struck deeper and deeper roots into the soil, gaining from the soil a spiritual strength which flowered into a continuous creation of brilliant religious value. . . . Even the ruthless might of imperial Rome was not able to shatter the physical and spiritual bond which linked the Jew to his land. The conqueror could strike coins and medals recording that Judaea was captive to Rome; but he could not strike out from the heart of the Jewish people that love of their land which had grown ever more closely intertwined with their heartstrings through the chastisements of their history and joys of their religion. . . . There was no hiatus in Jewish occupation in Palestine. There were always Jews in Palestine. . . . The basis of the traditional Prayer Book . . . the Mishna . . . the Palestinian Talmud. . . . The Masorah (storehouse of grammatical study safeguarding the letter of the text of the Hebrew Bible) . . . modern Hebrew poetry . . . much of the Midrash . . . the Targum (Aramaic translation of Bible) . . . in a word, all that is of the highest value in Jewish literary productivity during seven or more centuries after the supposed Roman destruction of Jewish life in Palestine, proves to be the creation of a Palestinian Jewry. . . . The crusaders did their merciless best to wipe out by massacre every trace of Jewish life in the ancient land of the Jews. But more than fire and sword of men's hate was needed to prevent Jews finding their way back to the land. . . . With the waning of the fire of the Crusaders, Jewish residence in the land of Palestine has been continuously and uninterruptedly growing. . . . From the passage of the Jordan under the leadership of Joshua 3,000 years ago, to this day, there has been an organic uninterrupted continuity of Jewish life in the land of Israel. This physical continuity of Jewish settlement in the land . . . substantiates physically the unquestioned spiritual claim of the Jew on his land of promise. It reveals the Jew as continuously in Palestine from of old, and the Christian and Moslem as of yesterday. It justifies Jewish immigration into Palestine today as a matter of right and not of sufferance." [2]

3. Zion in rites and festivals

"Judaism is saturated with Palestine. . . . The very Hebrew language of the Bible (and of the traditional Prayer Book used in the synagogue) is the ancient language of Palestine. . . . It was in Palestine that the Hebrew calendar which regulates Jewish life was established. The time table of Jewish life is set not by the meridian of Greenwich, but by that of Jerusalem. . . . Our three major festivals are reflections of meteorological conditions in Palestine. . . . *Tisha B'ab* and the minor fasts recall to the Jew the tragic days suffered in Palestine. . . . *Hanukah* rejoices at a Palestinian victory. The New Year of Trees, a festival which has taken on new meaning since the blossoming of Palestine in our own day, is celebrated in these climes in the heart of winter; it is Arbor Day in Palestine. . . . Page after page of the Prayer Book breathes the hope of Zion rebuilt, the gathering of her exiles and the reestablishing of Jewish life in its center in Palestine." [3]

"The oath which the first exiles pronounced at the streams of Babylon, Jews did not forget! Eras came and went, civilizations grew and decayed, empires rose and fell, historic trends flowed and ebbed, but Jerusalem was yet prized above all joys and remembered in all sorrows. Under the *Huppah* (the wedding canopy) when two hearts are beating in unison, when joy reigns supreme, there comes from the depth of the soul the prayer, 'May there soon be heard in the cities of Judah and in the streets of Jerusalem the voice of gladness, the voice of bridegroom and the voice of bride.' And when in the house of mourning sorrow oppresses the heart and longing tests faith, the lips murmur, 'He who fills the world, comfort ye together with all those that mourn for Zion and Jerusalem.' . . . And when death claimed the Jew and the cold earth opened its mouth, the head of the Jew rested on a bag of Palestinian soil." [4]

4. Never forgot Zion

"The Jew did not forget. In the midst of the luxury and the splendor of Artaxerxes' court, Nehemiah moved about like a shadow, his ears attuned to news 'about the Judean remnant that had survived the exile.' . . . A thousand years later, the Jews had not yet forgotten. In the Spanish metropolis, in Mohammedan Granada, city of culture, wealth and luxury, Samuel the prince, the vizier, was next to the king, the first man in the land. He enjoyed the respect, the admiration, the love of Jew and non-Jew. . . . His family had carved a nook for itself in the land of its adoption. But hearken to the abandoned cry of a dignified statesman, 'I weep bitterly with a trembling eye, and with a heavy spirit I murmur, as though the enemies' spear did my heart stab. O God! Will forever Christian and Arab ascend to the very stars, and the daughter of Zion sink to the depths of the Sea?' The Nehemiahs and the Samuels were not secular nationalists, political Zionists. They were men deeply religious and wherever they lived found shelter under the pinions of the *Shekinah*. Even the mystic author of that quaint, eclectic, Kabbalistic storehouse, the *Zohar*, saw in Palestine all beauty and all joy. He never forgot Palestine. It was forever to him the land of undying memories and spiritual opportunities. . . . Israel did not forget. Palestine was his dream. 'From the times of the prophets,' summarizes the great modern sage, Solomon Schechter, 'down to Judah Halevi in the twelfth century, and from the time of Judah Halevi down to the disciples of Elijah Vilna and Israel Baal Shem in the eighteenth and nineteenth centuries, (it) was always considered a country of great spiritual opportunities.' " [5]

5. Claim daily upheld

"If the Jewish people has earned the right to Palestine through its achievements there, it has doubly earned that land through its unswerving devotion to it after the exile. . . . The Jews have not omitted a single day in all the centuries that they have been dispersed among the nations, to reaffirm their right to national existence in Palestine. By that token the Jews have not merely upheld a claim in the face of forcible eviction; they have helped even in their absence to keep the land *spiritually* fruitful. The steadfast hope in their ultimate return to Palestine enabled the Jews to survive as a people. It has engendered whatever spiritual and cultural potentialities they still possess." [6]

6. An undying love

"Our love for Zion is one of our proudest titles. For no nation has ever loved its country with such a surpassing love as the people of Israel has loved the land of Israel. Though driven from Palestine nearly two thousand years ago, the Jewish people, which the world, knowing it only on the surface, considers a nation of hard-headed, sober-minded traders, has loved its ancient land with an undying love, with a romantic love, with a love one reads of in books of fiction, a love that expects no reward, a love that is happy in the privilege of loving. And yet, though expecting no reward, Israel received the amplest reward for its love. For it is this love which has enabled the Jewish people to survive until this day. The love of *Eretz Yisroel* was the torch that illumined the thorny path of our people. It was the anchor that kept our ship from drifting out into the boundless ocean. And when the eternal wanderer seemed to sink under the burden of his suffering, he looked up into the sky and saw the light that shone from Zion, and with renewed courage he continued on his journey." [7]

7. A creative force

"The Jewish problem has two aspects. . . . The material problem, the problem of discrimination, suffering, and persecution, must and will be solved by Jewish emancipation. But the spiritual problem, the problem of our higher destiny, will not, and cannot, be solved by Jewish emancipation. The solution of our material problem depends on the nations around us; the solution of our spiritual problem depends on our own endeavors. Now the spiritual problem of Jewry may be briefly formulated in these words: to make Judaism—not individual Jews, but our common Judaism—once more a creative force in the life of humanity. . . . In Palestine one man arose, single-handed, and in less than half a generation he performed a miracle: he resurrected a language

(Hebrew) which had not been spoken for two thousand years. . . . In the lands of the Dispersion we have hundreds of Jewish artists, many of them prominent in their fields, and yet we debate whether there is a Jewish art—and many deny it. But in Palestine a single man again, Boris Schatz, came and established the *Bezalel,* and laid the foundation at least for a Jewish art. . . . Palestine Jewry will take up the historic thread where it dropped . . . and perhaps if not we, then our children may live to see the fulfillment of the prophecy that the Law shall come forth out of Zion and the word of the Lord from Jerusalem." [8]

8. *The heart of Kelal Yisroel*

"But the significance of Palestine for the Jewries of the world lies still in another direction: it is the symbol of Israel's unity. . . . We speak of the *Kelal Yisroel,* the community of Israel . . . but who can say that the unity of Israel is real. True unity means unity of purpose, unity of hope; it means co-operation, give and take, equality and fellowship. Since the days of Jewish emancipation, Israel's unity, however, has consisted in the endeavor of the emancipated half to give succor to the unemancipated half. . . . What we need is a true unity, and there is no nobler unity than that of a common idea—a genuine Jewish life on a genuine Jewish soil. A portion of our people settled in the Holy Land, will prove a focus which will gather the efforts of all Jewries of the world, and it will prove at the same time a power-house which will send its energies to the whole house of Israel." [9]

9. *Zionism*

"Zionism means the establishment in Palestine of a Jewish National Home, publicly assured and legally secured." [10]

The Balfour Declaration, issued November 2, 1917, states: "His Majesty's Government views with favor the establishment in Palestine of a national home for the Jewish people, and will use their best endeavors to facilitate the achievement of this object, it being clearly understood that nothing shall be done which may prejudice the civil and religious rights of existing non-Jewish communities in Palestine, or the rights and political status enjoyed by Jews in any other country." The preamble to the mandate for Palestine to which not only Great Britain but the fifty-two nations then associated with the League, became partners, and which later received the endorsement of the United States Congress, adds the comment: "Recognition has thereby been given to the historical connection of the Jewish people with Palestine and to the grounds for reconstituting their national home in that country." Thus the ideal of Zionism has received the approval of the conscience of the nations of the world when that conscience was aroused and functioning.

"Whilst Zionism is constantly winning souls for the present, it is at the same time preparing for us the future. Only then, when Judaism has found itself, when the Jewish soul has been redeemed from the *Galuth*, can Judaism hope to resume its mission to the world. . . . The declaration, *Freedom is our Messiah*, which I have so often heard, may be good Fourth of July oratory, but it is miserably bad theology, and worse philosophy, having in view the terrible woes and complicated problems besetting humanity. Now, what happened once may happen again, and Israel may another time be called upon to fulfill its mission to the nations . . . but then Israel must first effect its own redemption and live again its own life, and be Israel again, to accomplish its universal mission. The passages in the Bible most distinguished for their universalistic tendency and grandeur are the verses in Isaiah and Micah, and there it is solemnly proclaimed: 'Out of Zion shall come forth the Law, and the word of the Lord from Jerusalem.' " [11]

10. Zionism and Religion

Some ultra-orthodox Jews object to Zionism because many of its exponents do not observe the traditional laws. But as a prominent Hassidic rabbi said: "I fail to understand those orthodox Jews who preach against Zionism because its leaders are not from the camp of the ultra-orthodox, and who believe it to be an act of impiety to associate with them. I ask: if the love of the Holy Land and the good deed, namely giving a dependable livelihood to many Jews, may be invalidated because of the partnership of less religious Jews, why should not the opposition to Zionism likewise be invalidated, inasmuch as the Reformers and assimilationists are partners and co-workers in agreement with you.

Hatred of Zion and abandonment of poor Jews—both impious matters —become virtues even when those who run away from Judaism share in them. On the other hand, love of Zion and helpfulness to the poor— both pious matters—become sins, because the less religious are aiding those who declare: 'We wish to be Jews.' " [12]

To the charge of a small group of rabbis—a minority of Reform rabbis who oppose the resolution of their convention endorsing Zionism, and who charge that Zionism is a secularist movement and is not in accord with the prophetic teachings, 733 rabbis representing every rabbinical organization in America issued a joint statement declaring that:

"Zionism is not a secularist movement. It has its origins and roots in the authoritative religious texts of Judaism. Scripture and rabbinical literature alike are replete with the promise of the restoration of Israel to its ancestral home. Anti-Zionism, not Zionism, is a departure from the Jewish religion. Nothing in the entire pronouncement of our colleagues is more painful than their appeal to the prophets of Israel—to those very prophets whose inspired and recorded words of national rebirth and restoration nurtured and sustained the hope of Israel throughout the ages.

"Nor is Zionism a denial of the universalistic teachings of Judaism. Universalism is not a contradiction of nationalism. Nationalism as such, whether it be English, French, American or Jewish, is not in itself evil. It is only militaristic and chauvinistic nationalism which shamefully flouts all mandates of international morality, which is evil. The prophets of Israel looked forward to the time not when all national entities would be obliterated, but when all nations would walk in the light of the Lord, live by His law and learn war no more.

"Our colleagues find themselves unable to subscribe to the political emphasis 'now paramount in the Zionist program.' . . . But even immigration and colonization are practical matters which require political action. The settlement of a half million Jews in Palestine since the last war was made possible by the political action which culminated in the Balfour Declaration and the Palestine Mandate. There can be little hope of opening the doors of Palestine for mass Jewish immigration after the war without effective political action. . . .

"Certainly our colleagues will allow to the Jews of Palestine the same rights that are allowed to all other peoples resident on their own land. If Jews should ultimately come to constitute a majority of the population of Palestine, would our colleagues suggest that all other peoples in the post-war world shall be entitled to political self-determination, whatever form that may take, but the Jewish people in Palestine shall not have such a right? Or do they mean to suggest that the Jews in Palestine shall forever remain a minority in order not to achieve such political self-determination? . . .

"Every fairminded American knows that American Jews have only one political allegiance—and that is to America. There is nothing in Zionism to impair this loyalty. Zionism has been endorsed by every President from Woodrow Wilson to Franklin Delano Roosevelt, and has been approved by the Congress of the United States. . . .

"The defeat of Hitler will not of itself normalize Jewish life in Europe. An allied peace which will not frankly face the problem of the national home-lessness of the Jewish people will leave the age-old tragic status of European Jewry unchanged. . . . Following the Allied victory, the Jews of Europe, we are confident, will be restored to their political rights and to equality of citizenship. But they possessed these rights after the last war and yet the past twenty-five years have witnessed a rapid and appalling deterioration of their position. In any case, even after peace is restored Europe will be so ravaged and war-torn that large masses of Jews will elect migration to Palestine as a solution of their personal problems. Indeed, for most of these there may be no other substantial hope of economic, social and spiritual rehabilitation."

11. The Jewish National Home and the Diaspora

"Volumes have been written upon its (Zionist) manifold aspects, the relation of the Jewish National Home in Palestine to Jewish dignity everywhere, the relation of a Jewish State to the protection of Jewish rights wherever Jews dwell, the influence which the Zionist movement has exerted in the last fifty years in reclaiming Jewish artists, scientists, men of letters and musicians, and the practical achievements in Palestine during the half century. . . . Much has been written and spoken of Palestine as the refuge which has absorbed more victims of German, Polish and Rumanian persecution than any other land, and of the way the Jewry of Palestine has met the years of Arab terror. . . . We are engaged in the task of building a Jewish nation and Jewish nationhood. . . . Let us look toward the day when an enlightened humanity will broaden its definitions of nationhood. In such a time, the Jewish National Home, or the Jewish State in Palestine, will serve not only as exemplar but as feeder of Jewish spiritual and cultural nourishment to Jewish communities wherever they may dwell. . . . Palestine is the heart of Jewish hope and promise. Zionsim is the spiritual dynamic of the Jewish people. It helps to give spiritual content to Jewish life everywhere." [13]

Questions for Discussion

1. What is meant by Political Zionism and Cultural Zionism? Can the two go together?
2. What is the Basle Program and the Balfour Declaration?
3. Is Nationalism opposed to Universalism?
4. Is Zionism unfair to the Arab people?
5. Can you conceive the continuity of Jewish life with Zion eradicated from the Jewish consciousness?
6. Discuss the implications of the "White Paper" and the "Biltmore Program."

CHAPTER XXXV

Charting the Way of Life

1. Jewish Wills and Testaments

If there is any place where a man wants to emphasize his ideals, it is in the final will and testament which he leaves for his children. The following quotations, culled from the Hebrew wills of Jewish fathers who lived in different countries and at different times, give us a general insight into ideals commonly cherished among Jews and held up by parents for the guidance of their children:

2. Science and religion, books and men

"My son, exert thyself while still young. . . . Devote thyself to science and religion. . . . As the Arabian philosopher holds, there are two sciences, ethics and physics; strive and excel in both. . . . Make thy books thy companions; let thy cases of books be thy pleasure gardens and grounds. Bask in their paradise, gather their fruit, pluck their roses, take their spices and their myrrh. . . . Enter into no dispute with the obstinate, not even on matters of Torah. . . . Show honor to thyself, thy household, and thy children by providing decent clothing as far as means allow. Spare from thy belly and put it on thy back. . . . Have a smile for all men. Though thou takest fees from the rich, heal the poor gratuitously. . . . Examine regularly, once a week, thy drugs and thy herbs. (He was a physician.) . . . Watch thy diet. Be content with little and good, and beware of hurtful sweets. . . . There is no more disgraceful object than a sick physician, who shall forsooth mend others when he cannot mend himself. . . . My son, I command thee to honor thy wife to thine utmost capacity. . . . Let thy words be gentle." [1]

166

3. *Humility*

"Accustom thyself to speak in gentleness to all men, at all times. Remove anger from thy heart, then there will arise in thy heart the quality of humility, better than all good things. . . . Understand, my son, that he who prides himself over other men is a rebel against the Kingship of Heaven. . . . Let thy eyes be turned earthwards and thy heart heavenwards. . . . In all thy doings, and thoughts, and at all times, regard thyself as one standing before the Omnipresent. . . . Read in the Torah regularly, so that thou mayest be able to fulfill its precepts, and when thou prayest remove all worldly considerations from thy heart. . . . Read this letter once a week." [2]

4. *Habitual goodness*

"Accustom yourselves to habitual goodness, for habit and character are closely interwoven, habit becomes second nature. Again, the perfection of the body is an antecedent to the perfection of the soul. . . . Avoid association with the company of the wanton, be found rather in the company of the learned but behave modestly in their presence. . . . Use refined phrases, let your utterance be clear, tranquil and to the point. . . . Love truth and righteousness. Hate falsehood and injustice. . . . Disdain reservations, subterfuges, tricks, sharp practices and evasions. Stand by your words, let not a legal contract or witnessed deed be more binding than your verbal promise, whether publicly or privately given. . . . Let your moral life be your pride of lineage, and your loyalty to truth your sufficient wealth, for there is no heritage equal to honor. . . . Be kind to the poor and the sorrow-stricken. Never cease to do good to all whom it is in your power to serve, and be on guard against working ill to any man whatsoever. Condemn idleness and loath ease. . . . Glory in forbearance, for that is real strength and true victory. . . . Make matter subject to mind. . . . Eat that you may live, and lay a ban on excess." [3]

5. The golden mean

"Be not prone to enter into quarrels; beware of oppressing fellowmen whether in money or word. Never feel envy or hate. . . . Never be weary of making friends, consider one enemy as one too many. . . . But entice no friendship by adulation and hypocrisy. Hold thyself firmly in the middle path in the satisfaction of thy appetites. So, be neither accessible to all, nor a recluse. Be faithful to all men irrespective of creed. Never give a fellowman cause for resentment. . . . Be ever responsive to the call of charity." [4]

6. Strict social and personal responsibility

"These are the things which my sons and daughters shall do at my request. They shall go to the house of prayer daily. . . . Their business must be conducted honestly with Jew and Gentile. They must be gentle in their manners. . . . They shall give an exact tithe of all their possessions. . . . If they can by any means contrive it, my children should live in communities, and not isolated from other Jews, so that their sons and daughters may learn the ways of Judaism. Even if compelled to solicit from others the money to pay a teacher, they must not let the young of both sexes go without instruction in the Torah. Marry your children young to members of respectable families. Let no child of mine hunt after money by making a low match for that object. . . . I command that the daughters of my house never be without work to do, for idleness leads first to boredom, then to sin. . . . Forbear and forgive. . . . In trade be true, never grasping at what belongs to another. . . . Give thanks for whatever favors come to you. Be grateful. . . . Judge every man charitably. . . . On festivals, seek to make happy the poor and needy. . . . As ye speak no scandal, so listen to none. . . . Have no funeral orations in my honor." [5]

7. A prayerful life

"Let each of you pray to God for a contrite and understanding heart from which ill-will and envy shall be far. Let each pray for sustenance that it may be won honestly without the crushing anxiety which drives out higher things. Above all, let each pray for loyalty and virtue in his offspring. Every day a different form of words must be used, lest by familiarity the prayers lose their spontaneity. . . . . Prayer is an inspiration for that purity of heart which shall inspire the service of God in love and reverence." [6]

8. Family love and moderation

"Keep yourself constantly from anger, falsehood, hatred, contention, envy and incontinence. . . . Show all honor to your mother. Live together in love and brotherliness and friendship. . . . You, husbands, honor your wives, and the latter shall on their part do full honor to their husbands, being to them a garland of roses, sweet flowers whose scent is Lebanon. . . . If your wealth increase, be not proud; unto the rich, more than others, is humility becoming. . . . Keep strict account of your expenditure, acting parsimoniously to yourself and generously to others. What you save from frivolous outlay, add bountifully to your charities. . . . I warn you against making promises for fulfillment at a future time. . . . With any religious duty never postpone its performance. . . . Keep careful accounts. Apply the same rule to your moral conduct. . . . Love work, hate the idleness which tires more than toil itself. Be kings, not slaves, to your passions. . . . If you render kindness to a person do not recurrently remind him of it. Fix ye this maxim in your hearts: *Do the good that you say,* but *say not the good that you do!*" [7]

Questions for Discussion

1. If you were to make a will of this kind, what would you advise your children to do or to avoid?
2. What special Jewish obligations would you ask them to assume?
3. What do you consider to be the behavior of a very fine person?

CHAPTER XXXVI

Looking Forward

1. A growing tradition

This Judaism of ours is not an inheritance that is handed down of itself, automatically, but it must *be made* the heritage of the congregation of Israel. . . . To make Judaism ours, that is our primal duty. Each one of us who takes part in this Jewish life of ours, who grasps firmly the Great Traditon and tries to carry it forward to new heights and to new achievement, may justly feel that he is worthy of that heritage, and is safeguarding its future. . . . Judaism must be enriched by our own spiritual experiences. . . . A living tradition is one that grows, that develops, that becomes richer and fuller because of further spiritual insight and experience. With the renascent Jewish life in Palestine we have reason to believe and to hope that a new chapter has begun in the life of the Jew and in the life of Judaism. . . . We cannot, however, and dare not depend upon that alone. If Jews are to take firm hold of this Tradition again, they must be awakened to their duty through knowledge—knowledge of the true meaning and significance of the Torah, of this Jewish Tradition. . . . For the Jew, the Tree of Life is *within* the Tree of Knowledge. . . . The Jew must learn to say again in the words of our ancestors standing at the foot of Sinai: *Na'ase Venishma!,* "We shall do and we shall *understand!"* [1]

2. A Gulf Stream among the nations

"Like the river that takes its rise in the distant hills, gradually courses its way through the country, passing alike through sublime landscape and hideous morass, offering its banks for the foundation of great cities, its waters enriched and modified by the tributaries that gradually flow toward it, until it at last loses itself in the ocean; so Judaism, taking its rise among the mountains of Sinai, slowly and steadily has advanced; passing alternately through a golden age of toleration and an iron age of persecution, giving its moral code for the foundation of many a government; modified by the customs and modes of life of each nation through which it passed, chastened and enriched by centuries of experience—shall we say, as was said with the river, that it, too, at last loses itself in the great sea of humanity? No! rather like the Gulf Stream, which, passing through a vast Atlantic Ocean, part of it, and yet distinct from it, never losing its individuality, but always detected by its deeper color and warmer temperature, until it eventually modifies the severe weather of distant country: so Judaism, passing through all the nations of the world, part of them and yet distinct from them, ever recognized by its depth and intensity, has at last reached this new world without having lost its individuality. And here it is still able, by the loftiness of its ethical truth and by the purity of its principles, to give intellectual and moral stamina to a never-ending future humanity." [2]

3. Birth and worth

"Being a Jew in the broadest definition means first, the accident of birth; secondly, the act of choice, choosing to remain Jewish despite the difficulties; thirdly, the act of cognition, learning to know the history and literature of his people so as to understand its soul and appreciate its place in the world; and finally, the act of transmission, transmitting to the next generation his heritage and the will to carry it on so that the Jewish people may not perish from the earth." [3] Being a Jew means being a Jew by worth as well as by birth. It means not only helping Israel to survive but helping it to survive on a spiritual and cultural plane worthy of its great historic tradition.

4. Glory of historic continuity

"It is our belief that the assimilation of the Jew is undesirable. Because he constitutes a minority he is compelled to think more and harder than his neighbor; he must be a liberal; his outlook must be international, his perspective universal. Assimilation would mean the absorption of such valuable assets in large crowds and majorities in no way superior. The Jew, too, is in many ways an indispensable factor in European civilization; he is an antidote for Western paganism; he is a force for universal peace. His continued existence is also a tremendous spiritual asset and means the cultural enrichment of our civilization.

"But above all, it has a profound esthetic appeal to the Jew himself and to the world. It is glorious to live, to roll up years, decades, centuries, millennia. It is thrilling to look back in vistas of time; there I was— then I was. Age, mere age, evokes interest, admiration and respect. A diamond wedding anniversary gets a headline in the newspaper. The celebration of the hundredth birthday of almost anyone arouses comment. Medicine is deeply interested in the prolongation of life. . . . An American need not go beyond his own country for natural beauty, but he travels to Rome, Jerusalem, Cairo to experience the old. . . . How pained we all are to see an old landmark, an age-hoary shrine disappear. Gibraltar is huge, massive, picturesque; some even declare it ugly, but there it stands. Suggest to anyone that it be reduced to the level of the sea and build with its stone magnificent cathedrals. No! We love to venerate the merely old.

"Here is the Jew—roll back the book of history; you are almost at its very beginning. Abraham was there to exchange compliments with Hammurabi. Turn a leaf; here is Rameses, well he had his difficulties with the God of the Hebrews, as we now know, and was the scion of a great people, but he is, after all, only a mummy. But even as a mummy, because it is so very old and has so admirably defied time, Rameses has attained a commendable reputation; but Moses, mind you, is no mummy and his burning bush is not yet consumed.

"Continue to turn the pages of history; new names, new cultures, new countries, new habits, new customs. The Jew, the Jew, he is yet there. . . . The firebrand which set on fire the Temple and reduced it to ashes, nineteen centuries ago, was hurled by one of Titus' soldiers from Mount Scopus. . . . The University of Jerusalem (is) built on the very mountain. . . . 'In social as in biological problems, time is the sole real creator and the sole great destroyer. It is time that has made mountains with grains of sand and raised the obscure cell of geological eras to human dignity.' Time has made the Jew. Time has thought him thus far desirable. Time alone will have to prove him undesirable." [4]

But, our tradition tells us, Abraham rose above the stars. The Jewish calendar was in the hands of the sages. We can, if we will, determine our place in time!

5. *Renewal of civilizing vitality*

"The efforts of all thoughtful Jews ought to be directed toward the renewal of the vitality of Judaism as a civilizing force. The attention of the rising generation of Jews, who are so frequently bewildered by the discrepancy between teaching and practice in the lives of those who claim to be religious and in the conduct of those who claim to be civilized, ought to be directed to the Jewish conception of life and interpretation of duty, to Jewish optimism and idealism, and to the Jewish sense of dependence upon the will of God, as expressed in Jewish teachings and illustrated in Jewish religious observance. Judaism will then have established its claim to be a safe guide through life and to form an integral part of all true culture. The Jewish people will then be in a position to renew its contribution to the solution of the world's problems, and to the establishment of a reign of peace, truth and justice. And the remnant of Jacob shall be in the midst of many peoples, as dew from the Lord, as showers upon the grass, that are not looked for from men, nor awaited at the hands of the sons of men." [5]

6. *Continuity and growth*

"We have the forward-looking gaze. We wish to see a development in Jewish thought and practice. But . . . we cannot consider any change in Judaism which would mean cutting ourselves away from catholic Israel and severing our connection with the continuity of Jewish *historical* development. As modern thinking men and women we realize the necessity of harmonizing traditional Judaism with modern thought, and of employing new categories by which the substance of old doctrines are to be stated to the intellectual satisfaction of our generation." [6]

7. Conscious evolution

"For Judaism to become creative once again, it must assimilate the best in contemporary civilizations. In the past this process of assimilating cultural elements from the environment was carried on unconsciously. Henceforth that process will have to be carried on in deliberate and planned fashion. . . .

"The criterion which is to determine whether a suggested change is beneficial or detrimental to Judaism is the extent to which it helps Judaism to retain its *continuity*, its *individuality* and its *organic character*. . . . To render Judaism creative it is essential to redefine the national status and reorganize the communal life of the Jews. Fundamental to the reorganization of Jewish life is national unity. That unity is not determined by geographic boundaries; it is cultural rather than political. The Jews are an international nation, functioning as such by virtue of their consciousness of a common past, their aspirations toward a common future and the will to cooperate in the achievement of common ends.

"Palestine should serve as the symbol of the Jewish renascence and the center of Jewish civilization—Jewish communal life is the *sine qua non* of cooperation among Jews. In America, particularly, Jews will need a measure of communal autonomy if American-Jewish life is to develop along broad and inclusive lines. Jewish organization should embrace all the activities of Jews, and integrate those activities into an organic unity. To such communities will belong all Jews who feel physical or spiritual kinship with the Jewish people, no matter what their personal philosophy may be. . . .

"True to his historic tradition he (the Jew) should throw in his lot with all movements to further social justice and universal peace, and bring to bear on them the inspiration of his history and religion." [7]

8. Relief, Zion and disciplined Jewish life

"Relief, Zion rebuilt and Jewish education, are therefore the most urgent duties of this grave hour. Whatever communal organization need be effected, whatever institutions need be built in order to enable us to fulfill these duties, should command the support of every Jew. These will not solve all our problems. They will not eradicate hate from the hearts of our unreasoning enemies. That belongs to the task which eternity imposes upon us. . . . As long as flagrant economic inequalities will continue, as long as false ideals and standards will rule men's minds, as long as the violence of the wicked will not be resisted courageously by men of good will, human society will be unstable. Not only Israel, but all peoples will be insecure no matter what they may do in their own behalf. But obviously while these problems have a direct effect upon our welfare, we cannot with our own limited powers ever hope to solve them. . . . These problems we share together with men of good will of all races, nations, creeds, and colors. . . . To that extent our destiny and mankind's destiny are one and inseparable. . . . In the tasks of relief, Zionism and Jewish education, however, we need not wait for anyone else. They depend upon our understanding and determination. If we devote ourselves wholeheartedly to them we will be preparing ourselves most effectively for the role we are to play in the tasks facing mankind as a whole. Only a Jewish mind rooted in Jewish wisdom, a Jewish soul purified by Jewish ideals, and a Jewish life disciplined by Jewish law, can make a maximum contribution to the solution of the essentially ethical and moral questions plaguing modern society." [8]

9. *Ideal American Jew*

"When we try to penetrate the mist that encircles the horizon of the present, a vision unfolds itself before our mind's eye, presenting a picture of the future of American Israel. We perceive a community great in numbers, mighty in power, enjoying life, liberty and the pursuit of happiness: true life, not mere breathing space; full liberty, not mere elbow room; real happiness, not that of pasture beasts; actively participating in the civic, social and economic progress of the country, fully sharing and increasing its spiritual possessions and acquisitions, doubling its joys, halving its sorrows; yet deeply rooted in the soil of Judaism, clinging to its past, working for its future, true to its traditions, faithful to its aspirations, one in sentiment with their brethren wherever they are, attached to the land of their fathers as the cradle and resting place of the Jewish spirit; men with straight backs and raised heads, with big hearts and strong minds, with no conviction crippled, with no emotion stifled, with souls harmoniously developed, self-centered and self-reliant; receiving and resisting, not yielding like wax to every impress from the outside, but blending the best they possess with the best they encounter; not a horde of individuals, but a set of individualities, adding a new note to the richness of American life, leading a new current into the stream of American civilization; not a formless crowd of taxpayers and voters, but a sharply marked community, distinct and distinguished, trusted for its loyalty, respected for its dignity, esteemed for its traditions, valued for its aspirations, a community such as the Prophet of the Exile saw it in his vision: 'And marked will be their seed among the nations, and their offspring among the peoples. Everyone that will see them will point to them as a community blessed by the Lord.' " [9]

Notes and References

I. Starting the Day Right

1. Traditional Morning Prayer.
2. Standard Prayer Book, p. 5.
3. *Ibid.*, p. 7 f.
4. *Ibid.*, p. 8.
5. *Peah.*, Ch. I; *ibid.*, p. 5.

II. God

1. Ps., XIV, 1.
2. Ps., XIX.
3. Ex. R., V, 14.
4. Evening Prayer.
5. Ps., CIV.
6. Daily Morning Prayer.
7. Gen. R., VI, 4.
8. Deut., XXX, 15–20.
9. Ex., XXXIV, 6–7.
10. Gen. R., XII, 15.
11. Ex., XXII, 21.
12. Prov., XIV, 31.
13. San., 103a.
14. Yoma, 23a.
15. Tosefta, *Shebuot*, III, 6.
16. *Zohar*, Trans. by Sperling & Simon, Vol. I, p. 44.

III. The Problem of Evil

1. Ex., XXXIII, 12 f.
2. Job, IX, 22–4.
3. *Ibid.*, XXXIII, 14 f.
4. Jer., XII, 1–2.
5. Ps., LXXIII.
6. Abr. Ibn Daud, *The Sublime Faith*, Pt. II, Princ. 6, Ch. II.

7. Maimonides, *The Guide for the Perplexed*.
8. Sifre, Deut. 33.
9. Ber., 5a.
10. Gen. R., XXXII, 3.
11. *Zohar,* Trans. Meyer, p. 337.
12. Judah Halevi, *The Kusari*.
13. Jos. Albo, *Sefer Haikkarim*.
14. J. H. Hertz, *Book of Jewish Thoughts*, p. 297.

IV. Man

1. Sifra, *Kedoshim*.
2. ADN, XXXI.
3. San., 37a.
4. Gen. R., VIII, II.
5. Jos. Albo, *Sefer Haikkarim*.
6. Abot, III, 14. See Herford, Abot, III, 18.
7. Abot, II, 1.
8. *Ibid.,* LV, 1.
9. Zerahia, *Sefer Hayashar,* p. 28.
10. Judah Halevi, *The Kusari*.
11. Taanit, 22a.
12. Jer. Kid., IV.
13. Tanhuma, 58.
14. Judah'Halevi, *Kusari,* II.
15. Mechilta, XX, 21.
16. Sota, 4b.
17. Abot, V, 6.
18. Erub., 54a.
19. Abot, VI, 6.
20. *Ibid.,* IV, 12.
21. San., 36a.

V. Mercy

1. Sab., 133b.
2. ADN, XXXV, 2.
3. *The Will of Zebulun,* V, 1, quoted in Roth, *Hadeot Ve-Hamidot,* p. 18.
4. Meg., 10.
5. Notes from a lecture by Prof. Ginzberg.
6. Jer. Jeb., XV.

7. Git., 62a.

8. Gen. R., XXXIII.

VI. Faith

1. Mak., 24a.
2. Sota, 48b.
3. Taan., 21a.
4. Ber., 60a.
5. Pes., 64a.
6. Ket., 30a.
7. Newman, *Hassidic Anthology*, pp. 103–4.
8. *Ibid.*
9. *Ibid.*
10. *Ibid.*, pp. 104–5.
11. *Ibid.*, p. 107.
12. M. Lipson, *Die Welt Derzeilt*, Vol. I, p. 166.

VII. Prayer

1. M. Joseph, *Judaism as Creed and Life*, pp. 340 ff.
2. *Ibid.*
3. Abot, II, 18.
4. Ber., 28b.
5. Jeb., 105b.
6. Proverb quoted in Schechter, *Some Aspects of Rabbinic Theology*, p. 157.
7. Cf. Schechter, *ibid.*, pp. 228–9.
8. *Zohar*, Trans. Sperling & Simon, Vol. IV, p. 181.
9. J. H. Hertz, *Book of Jewish Thoughts*, p. 196.
10. Deut., VI, 4–9.
11. M. Lipson, *Die Welt Derzeilt*, Vol. 2, p. 100.
12. Newman, *Hassidic Anthology*, pp. 334–41.
13. Morning Prayer, Standard Edit., pp. 7–8.
14. *Ibid.*, p. 91.
15. Prayer concluding each service, *ibid.*, p. 94.
16. *Zohar, Vayakhel*. Recited before taking out the Scroll, *ibid.*, p. 208.
17. Prayer after reading of Torah on Sabbath morning, *ibid.*, p. 218.
18. Ber., 16b. Recited on Sabbath before the new month, *ibid.*, pp. 219–20.
19. New Year Day Prayer, *ibid.*, pp. 350–1.
20. Bachya Ibn Pakuda, *The Duties of the Heart*. Recited by many on the eve of Yom Kippur.

VIII. The Synagogue

1. K. Kohler, quoted in Hertz, *Book of Jewish Thoughts,* p. 189.
2. Ber., 8a.
3. *Ibid.*
4. *Ibid.,* 47b.
5. Sab., 11a.
6. M. Joseph, *Judaism as Creed and Life,* pp. 287–8.
7. Ch. N. Bialik, transl. by Maurice Samuel.
8. M. M. Kaplan, *Judaism as a Civilization,* pp. 426–8.
9. *Ibid.,* p. 428.

IX. Torah

1. Abot, II, 6.
2. *Ibid.,* I, 1.
3. Pes., 68b.
4. Gen. R., VIII, 2.
5. Sab., 88a.
6. A.Z., 3b.
7. Ps., XIX, 8–10.
8. Deut. R., VIII, 6.
9. Abot, V, 24.
10. *Ibid.,* I, 15.
11. *Ibid.,* II, 17.
12. *Ibid.,* IV, 18.
13. *Ibid.,* VI, 4.
14. *Ibid.,* VI, 6.
15. *Ibid.,* III, 3, 4.
16. *Ibid.,* I, 4.
17. San., 91b.
18. *Ibid.,* 19b.
19. Nid., 81a.
20. ADN, II.
21. Sab., 119b.
22. Abot, IV, 25.
23. Abot, IV, 1.
24. San., 99a.
25. Lev. R., III.
26. Abot, II, 6.
27. *Ibid.,* III, 21.
28. *Ibid.,* V, 10.

29. L. Ginzberg's *Students, Scholars and Saints*, pp. 42 f.
30. *Ibid.*, pp. 14–15.
31. Compare S. Schechter, *Studies in Judaism*, p. 296.
32. I. Friedlaender, *Past and Present*, p. 289, Note 2.
33. *Ibid.*, pp. 287 f.
34. *Ibid.*, pp. 288–9.
35. Abot, II, 17.
36. A.Z., 17a.
37. Ber., 17a.
38. Deut. R., VII.
39. Ber., 11b; Morning Prayer, Standard Prayer Book, p. 4.

X. *Mitzvoth*

1. Prov., III, 17.
2. Makkoth, 23b.
3. See Schechter, *Some Aspects of Rabbinic Theology*, pp. 138 f.
4. Tos, Sab., XV.
5. Gen. R., Chap. 48.
6. Sota, 31b.
7. Abot, IV, 2.
8. L. I. Newman, *Hassidic Anthology*, p. 266.
9. *Ibid.*
10. Abr. Ibn Ezra, *Yesod Mora*, pp. 27 f.
11. Abr. of Barzilonah, *Sefer Ha-Hinuk*, p. 3.
12. Abot, II, 5.
13. D. Aronson, *R.A.A. Proceedings*, Vol. VI, pp. 150–3.

XI. *Truth*

1. Abot, I, 18.
2. San., 24b.
3. Pes., 113.
4. Makk., 24a.
5. Sab., 104a.
6. Newman, *Hassidic Anthology*, p. 487.
7. *Ibid.*, pp. 488–9.
8. Sota, 41a.
9. Newman, *ibid.*
10. Sota, 22a.
11. See Gen. R., LXV.

12. Tosefta, B.K., VII, 8.

13. Suk, 46b.

14. Newman, *Hassidic Anthology,* p. 511.

15. *Ibid.*

16. *Ibid.,* p. 493.

17. L. Ginzberg, quoted in M. Kadushin, *Organic Thinking,* p. 306, Note 276.

18. Newman, *Hassidic Anthology,* p. 511.

19. Arach, 15b.

20. ADN, XV.

21. *Ibid.*

22. Pirke D'Rabbi Eliezar, 53.

23. Pesak, 118a.

24. Shab., 33a.

25. San., 68b.

26. Newman, *Hassidic Anthology,* p. 512.

27. Ket., 5a.

28. Newman, *ibid.,* p. 510.

XII. Justice

1. Deut., XVI, 20.

2. Deut. R., V, 1.

3. Ex. R., XXX; Sifra, 91a; See Schechter, *Some Aspects of Rabbinic Theology,* pp. 229–30.

4. San., 7b.

5. Ket., 105b.

6. B.K., 83b f.

7. Newman, *Hassidic Anthology.*

8. A. Geiger, quoted in Hertz, *Book of Jewish Thoughts,* p. 32.

XIII. Peace

1. Micha, IV, 1–4.

2. Taan., 68a.

3. Peah, Chap. I, Mishna 1.

4. San., 38a.

5. *Ibid.,* 22a.

6. *Ibid.,* 7a.

7. Statement by the Rabbinical Assembly of America of its Peace Objectives.

XIV. Charity and Social Service

1. Abot, III, 8.
2. Git., 7b.
3. Lev. R., XXXIV, 8.
4. B.B., 10a.
5. Shab., 151b.
6. B.B., 9a.
7. Lev. R., XXXIV, 9.
8. Lev. R., XXXIV, 4.
9. B.B., 9b.
10. Ket., 67a.
11. Ib., 67b.
12. Maimonides, *Mishneh Torah,* Bk. 7, Chap. X, 7–14. Joseph Caro included it in his *Shulhan Aruch,* Article 249, Sec. 6 ff.
13. Caro, *Shulhan Aruch,* Art. 248–9.
14. *Ibid.,* Art. 251, Sec. 8 f.
15. Sota, 49b.
16. Abot, I, 1.
17. Newman, *Hassidic Anthology,* pp. 40–41.
18. *Ibid.,* p. 35.
19. E. Fleg. *The Jewish Anthology,* trans., by M. Samuel, pp. 348–52.

XV. Hospitality

1. Taan., 20b.
2. Abot, I, 15.
3. American Jewish Year Book, Vol. 43, p. 549.
4. *Ibid.,* p. 577.

XVI. Labor

1. Abot., II, 2.
2. Psalm, CXXVIII, 2.
3. Berak, 8a.
4. Abot, I, 10.
5. Ket., 59b.
6. Kid., 29a.
7. Maimonides, quoted in I. H. Levinthal, *Judaism,* p. 217.
8. Berak, 8a.
9. Ned., 49b.

10. *Ibid.*
11. Pes., 113a.
12. Eccles. R., IX, 9.

XVII. Employer and Employee

1. Lev., XIX, 13.
2. Mishna, B.M., VII, 1.
3. Ex. R., XIII, 1.
4. B.M., 38a.
5. B.M., 77a, b. See Levinthal, *Judaism,* pp. 238–9.
6. Levinthal, *ibid.,* p. 240.

XVIII. Business Standards

1. Mech., 46a.
2. Shab., 31a.
3. Lev., XIX, 35.
4. Mishna, B.B., V, 10.
5. B.B., 61b.
6. *Ibid.,* 89a.
7. *Ibid.,* 90b.
8. Pes., 113b.
9. Ruth R., III, 18.
10. Tosefta, B.K., VII, 8.
11. Deut. R., CXI, 3.

XIX. The Good Life

1. Beza, 32b.
2. Jer. Ber., IX.
3. Shab., 118a.
4. Erub., 18a.
5. Abot, II, 5.
6. Ber., 58a.
7. Lev. R., IV, 6.
8. Abot, II, 1.

XX. The Good Society

1. Rabbinical Assembly of America, Pronouncement, 1934, published in Religion and the Good Society, edit. by B. Y. Landis, p. 41.
2. Central Conference of American Rabbis, 1928, *ibid.,* p. 41.

3. *Ibid.*, p. 40.
4. *Ibid.*, p. 42.
5. *Ibid.*, p. 45.
6. R.A.A., *ibid.*, p. 45.
7. *R.A.A. Proceedings*, Vol. VI, p. 84, E. Kohn.
8. B. Y. Landis, *Religion and the Good Society*, p. 43.
9. *Ibid.*, p. 47.
10. C.C.A.R., *ibid.*, p. 46.
11. *Ibid.*, p. 49.
12. *R.A.A. Proceedings*, Vol. VI, p. 831.
13. B. Y. Landis, *ibid.*, p. 56.
14. *R.A.A. Proceedings*, Vol. VI, p. 175.
15. *R.A.A.*, B. Y. Landis, *ibid.*, p. 52.
16. *Ibid.*, p. 55.

XXI. Leaders

1. Tanhuma, *Mishpatim*.
2. Sifre D., 13 f. Tanhumuh, *Behala'aloteka*. Cf. Jer. Peah, VII.
3. Cf. Ginzberg, *Legends*, Vol. III, p. 249.
4. R.H., 25a.
5. Schechter, *Seminary Addresses*, p. 20.
6. *Ibid.*, p. 116.
7. Newman, *Hassidic Anthology*, pp. 217–18.
8. *Ibid.*, p. 282.
9. Berakot, 28b.
10. Kaplan, *Judaism as a Civilization*, p. 81.
11. *Ibid.*, pp. 397–8.

XXII. The Use and Abuse of Money

1. A.Z., 5b.
2. Erub., 41b.
3. Pesak., 113b.
4. Abot, II, 6.
5. *Ibid.*, II, 8.
6. Moed K., 28.
7. Kohelet R., I.
8. *Ibid.*, V, 14.
9. Abot, IV, 1.
10. Erub., 65b.

11. Newman, *Hassidic Anthology,* pp. 271 f.
12. S. Ansky, *The Dybbuk.*

XXIII. *The Spirit and the Letter*

1. San., 106b.
2. Sifre, 131b. See Schechter, *Aspects of Jewish Theology,* p. 159 f.
3. Schechter, *ibid.,* p. 162.
4. Mid. Tehillim, CXIX: 1, 6. Ed. Buber, CXIX, 1:5.
5. Moore, *Judaism,* Vol. 2, pp. 320–21.
6. H. G. Enelow, "Kawwanah," in Studies in Jewish Literature, Kohler Anniversary Volume, pp. 82–107.
7. Bachya, *Duties of the Heart,* Introduction.
8. Maimonides, "Yad," Teshubah, XI.
9. Mishna, Bezah, beginning.
10. Kid., 49b.
11. L. Ginzberg, *Students, Scholars and Saints,* pp. 118–20.

XXIV. *The Family*

1. Isa. XLV, 15.
2. Jeb., 62a, b.
3. Mishna, *Yoma,* I, 1.
4. K. Kohler, *Jewish Theology,* pp. 316–17.
5. J. H. Hertz, *Affirmations of Judaism,* pp. 69, 72–3.
6. Tana d'be Eliyahu, p. 289.
7. M. Joseph, *Judaism as Creed and Life,* p. 403.

XXV. *Husband and Wife*

1. Gen. R., LXVIII, 4.
2. Jeb., 63a.
3. *Ibid.,* 62b.
4. Mishna, *Joma,* I, 1.
5. B.B., 8a; Sota, 44a.
6. San., 76a, b; Jeb., 101b.
7. Kid., 70a.
8. Sota, 2a.
9. Bech., 45b.
10. Pes., 49a.
11. Jeb., 63a.
12. Hul., 84b.

13. Sota, 17a. For a general discussion of the position of the Jewish woman, see D. Aronson, *Woman's Position in Israel,* in the Jewish Forum, Aug., and Oct., 1922.

XXVI. Marriage

1. M. M. Kaplan, *Judaism as a Civilization,* p. 436.
2. Standard Prayer Book, pp. 443–4.
3. Kaplan, *ibid.,* p. 420.
4. *Ibid.,* p. 422.

XXVII. Parental Responsibilities

1. Tacitus, *Histories,* V, 5.
2. Hertz, *Affirmations of Judaism,* pp. 69 f.
3. Yalkut, Prov., 964.
4. Kid., 40a.
5. Shab., 10b.
6. Exod. R., I, 1; M.K., 17a.
7. Git., 6b.
8. Shir. R., I, 4.
9. Suk., 42a.
10. Abot, IV, 25.
11. This and subsequent quotations are taken from I. Goldfarb, *The Jewish Lullaby,* in L. Jung edition. The Jewish Library Series, 3.
12. I. H. Levinthal, *Steering or Drifting,* p. 59.

XXVIII. Filial Duties

1. Jer. Peah, 15d.
2. Mishna, Peah, I, 1.
3. Kid., 31b.
4. Jer. Peah, 15c.
5. *Ibid.*
6. Kid., 31a.
7. Cf. *Ibid.,* 31b.
8. Sefer Hassidim, 152; Jer. Peah, I, 5.

XXIX. The Jewish Home

1. Num. XXV, 5.
2. J. Jacobs, *Jewish Ideals,* p. 12.
3. Condensed from Hertz, *Affirmations of Judaism,* pp. 79–81.

4. B. D. Greenberg, *The Jewish Home Beautiful,* pp. 13, 14.

5. I. R. Wolff, *The Jewish Woman in the Home,* in Jung edition, The Jewish Library Series, 3, pp. 94–5.

6. *Ibid.,* pp. 96–7.

7. Kaplan, *Judaism as a Civilization,* pp. 416–17.

8. *Ibid.,* p. 422.

XXX. Sabbath: A People's Cultural Dynamo

1. Schechter, *Some Aspects of Rabbinic Theology,* pp. 152 f.

2. Shab., 10b.

3. Jer. Nedarim, III.

4. Shir HaShirim R.

5. Gen. R., XI.

6. Shab., 119a.

7. Judah Halevi, transl. by S. Solis-Cohen, quoted in Millgram, *Anthology of Mediaeval Hebrew Literature,* pp. 44–45.

8. Solomon Halevi Alkabetz. See Standard Prayer Book, pp. 155–6. Quotation is a free translation by S. Solis-Cohen.

9. Traditional Sabbath Hymn. For translation see Goldman and Coopersmith, *Songs and Readings,* p. 304.

10. Shab., 119b.

11. Greenberg and Silverman, *The Jewish Home Beautiful,* p. 65.

12. M. M. Kaplan, *Judaism as a Civilization,* pp. 11–12.

13. M. Joseph, *Judaism as Creed and Life,* pp. 203 f.

14. Halevi, *Kusari,* III, 5.

15. Zohar, *Vayakhel.*

16. C. G. Montefiore, *The Bible for Home Reading,* M. Joseph, *ibid.,* p. 207.

17. Newman, *Hassidic Anthology,* p. 405.

18. Kaplan, *ibid.,* pp. 455–6 and p. 430.

XXXI. A Chosen People

1. Gen., XII, 1–3.

2. Gen., XIX, 19.

3. Amos, IX, 7.

4. Isaiah, XLII, 5–7.

5. Ex. R., I, 1.

6. Berak., 5a.

7. Sifre, Deut. 343, 142b. See *Ginzberg, Legends,* Vol. III, pp. 80 f.

8. Halevi, *Kusari*, II, Chap. 29 f.
9. Maimonides, *Mishneh Torah*, A.Z., I.
10. *Ibid., Abadim*, IX, 8.
11. Moses Mendelssohn, *Jerusalem*, pp. 72 f.
12. Schechter, *Some Aspects of Rabbinic Theology*, p. 62.
13. Mechilta, 102a.
14. Tanhuma, Noah, 19.
15. Schechter, *ibid.*, p. 64.
16. Joseph, *Judaism as Creed and Life*, p. 155.
17. Kohler, *Jewish Theology*, pp. 324-5.
18. Evening Prayer.
19. Morning Prayer. Cf. Ber., 11b.
20. Kaplan, *Judaism as a Civilization*, pp. 409-14.

XXXII. *Jew and Non-Jew*

1. Tosef., San., XIII, 2; Maimonides, *Yad*, Hil. Teshubah, III, 5.
2. Sifra to XVIII, 5.
3. Suk., 55b.
4. I Kings, VIII, 41-43.
5. Tana d'be Eliyahu R, VIII.
6. Maimonides, *Yad*, Hil. Shemita, 13:13.
7. Meg., 9b.
8. Abraham b. Hiya of Barzilonah, *Sefer HaMussar*, Chap. I.
9. Ber., 58a.
10. Isaiah, II, 2; Micha, IV, 3.
11. L. Jung, *Judaism in a Changing World*, pp. 97 f.
12. Hullin, 13b.
13. A.Z., 65a.
14. Git., 50b, 51a.
15. San., 39b.
16. Maimonides, *Yad*, Hil. Melakim, 8, 10, 11.
17. B. Drachman, in Jung, *Judaism in a Changing World*, p. 114.
18. Isaac b. Sheshet, 14th Cent., Resp. 119.
19. Isaac Aramah, *Akedat Yitzhok*, 60:36.
20. Rabbi Jacob Emden, Cf. Jung, *ibid.*, pp. 121-36.
21. Quoted in Hertz, *Book of Jewish Thoughts*, p. 26.
22. Michael Guttmann, *Das Judentum und seine Umwei.*, Jung, *ibid.*, pp. 121-36.
23. I. Goldstein, *Toward a Solution*, pp. 61-3.

XXXIII. Nationalism

1. Emunot VeDeot, III, 7.
2. Schechter, *Some Aspects of Rabbinic Theology*, pp. 105–6.
3. *Ibid., Seminary Addresses*, p. 249.
4. Kaplan, *Judaism as a Civilization*, p. 253.
5. *Ibid.*, pp. 254–5.
6. I. Friedlaender, *Past and Present*, pp. 15–16.
7. *Ibid.*, pp. 33–4.

XXXIV. The Homeland

1. David de Sola Pool, in Jung, *The Jewish Library*, Series II, pp. 135–8.
2. *Ibid.*, pp. 139–44.
3. *Ibid.*, pp. 145–49.
4. S. Goldman, *A Rabbi Takes Stock*, p. 185.
5. *Ibid.*, pp. 186–7.
6. Kaplan, *Judaism as a Civilization*, p. 274.
7. I. Friedlaender, *Past and Present*, p. 471.
8. *Ibid.*, pp. 471–4.
9. *Ibid.*, pp. 474–6.
10. Basle Program, the official program of the World Zionist Organization.
11. Schechter, *Seminary Addresses*, pp. 103–4.
12. Newman, *Hassidic Anthology*, p. 302.
13. I. Goldstein, *Toward a Solution*, pp. 175–6.

XXXV. Charting the Way of Life

1. Judah Ibn Tibbon, Spain, 12th Century. (This and the following excerpts are taken from *Hebrew Ethical Wills*, edit. by I. Abrahams, Jewish Publication Society), Vol. I, pp. 54 f.
2. Nahmanides, 13th Cent. *Ibid.*
3. Attributed to Maimonides, 13th Cent., *ibid.*, pp. 103–5.
4. Asher b. Yehiel, 14th Cent., Germany, *ibid.*, pp. 118 f.
5. Eliazar of Mayence, 14th Cent., Vol. II, pp. 208 f.
6. Jonah b. Elijah Landsofer, 18th Cent., Prague, *ibid.*, pp. 287 f.
7. Elijah b. Raphael de Veali, 18th Cent., Italy, *ibid.*, pp. 303 f.

XXXVI. Looking Forward

1. Levinthal, *Judaism*, pp. 259 f.
2. M. H. Harris, quoted in Hertz, *Book of Jewish Thoughts*, pp. 41–2.

3- I. Goldstein, *Toward a Solution*, p. 85.
4- S. Goldman, *A Rabbi Takes Stock*, pp. 68–70.
5- Salis Daiches, in Jung, *Judaism in a Changing World*, pp. 252–3.
6- M. H. Farbridge, *Judaism and the Modern Mind*, pp. 293–4.
7- M. M. Kaplan, *Judaism as a Civilization*, pp. 514 f.
8- Simon Greenberg, *Living as a Jew Today*, pp. 94, 115 f.
9- I. Friedlaender, *Past and Present*, pp. 277–8.

CPSIA information can be obtained
at www.ICGtesting.com
Printed in the USA
LVHW070423070623
749020LV00006B/190